Becki
as told to Rhonda Graham

Best for Me

Pacific Press Publishing Association
Boise, Idaho
Oshawa, Ontario, Canada

Edited by Marvin Moore
Designed by Tim Larson
Cover photo © Parker Portraits
Typeset in 11/13 Century Schoolbook

Copyright © 1991 by
Pacific Press Publishing Association
Printed in the United States of America
All Rights Reserved

Library of Congress Cataloging-in-Publication Data:
Trueblood, Becki, 1963-
    Best for me : Becki pursues the Miss America crown
and faces the challenges of faith and fame / Becki Trueblood ; as told to Rhonda Graham.
        p.   cm.
    Summary: The author describes how she came to under-
stand God's will after not winning the Miss America contest.
    ISBN 0-8163-1050-5
    1. Trueblood, Becki, 1963- . 2. Beauty contestants—
United States—Biography—Juvenile literature. 3. Beauty
contests—United States—Juvenile literature. 4. Beauty
contestants—United States—Religious life—Juvenile literature. [1. Trueblood, Becki, 1963- . 2. Beauty contestants.
3. Beauty contests. 4. Christian life.] I. Graham, Rhonda.
II. Title.
HQ1220.U5T78 1991
791.6—dc20   91-13469
                                                  CIP
                                                  AC

91 92 93 94 95 • 5 4 3 2 1

Contents

Dedication:

**To My Brother, Todd,
I love you**

O Lord,
You know what is best
  for me.
Let this or that be done
  as You please.
Give what You will,
How much You will
And when You will.

—Thomas à Kempis (1380-1471)

Chapter 1

The Calling

I took my seat with the rest of the Heritage Singers as the lights in the auditorium dimmed. We'd sounded good—a nice, tight blend. I smiled, remembering the enthusiasm the young crowd greeted us with when we came on stage.

". . . would like to thank Max Mace and the Heritage Singers . . ."

I listened briefly to the announcer on stage, then tuned him out again. It felt so good to sit and relax after forty-five minutes of singing. I mentally ran through our schedule for the rest of the week. At least we had two days without a performance to relax and recuperate.

The man on stage continued talking. ". . . and now I'd like you to welcome Miss America 1987, Kellye Cash!"

The audience burst into applause as Kellye stepped on the stage. Picking up a microphone, she greeted everyone. The room fell silent. I looked around me, amazed. I'd never heard a youth festival audience get this quiet for anyone or anything.

"I'm excited to be here today," Kellye began. "The Lord has given me many chances to speak to non-Christian audiences in my year as Miss America, but there's something extra special about being with other Christians."

I watched her carefully. She looked pretty, but not particularly glamorous. I'd always thought of Miss America as something of a queen—someone who'd been trained since birth in talent and charm classes. Kellye looked like a regular person—a *beautiful* regular person.

". . . and the Lord blessed me with the opportunity to reach so many people this year. He used my year as Miss America to bring glory to His name." Kellye stopped and smiled at the audience before continuing.

"What a wonderful way to reach people," I thought as I watched her. In her position, she'd have so many opportunities to speak to those who normally wouldn't listen to anything about God. I admired her for it. I'd never imagined a beauty queen would have anything important to say. They seemed too airy, too preoccupied with their looks. "Maybe that's why people listen to her," I thought. "She breaks down their preconceptions and *makes* them listen."

". . . I grew up in a military family. We moved a lot and I had to find strength within myself to succeed . . ."

I thought of my own family. My parents always supported and believed in me. We'd lived in southern California most of my life, but moved to Caldwell, Idaho, right after I turned fifteen. My parents helped me survive the move and gave me lots of extra love as I adjusted to a new school and a whole new group of friends. And they'd been supportive when I'd decided to leave college and join the Heritage Singers. I could almost hear my mother's voice: "Whatever you want to be, you can be, Becki," she said. "When you accept God's will in your life, He will give you the desires of your heart, if your desires are right."

I watched Kellye finish her talk and walk off stage. Could I ever do anything like that? All my life I had felt God was preparing me for something. Even my experiences with Heritage made me feel I was in preparation for something. And for the last few months I knew God was leading me into a change. Could this be it? Could all the performing and speaking be leading to this? Did God want me to be Miss America?

As soon as the thought formed, I pushed it out of my mind. People would think I was doing it for my glory, I reminded myself. And besides, I told myself firmly, you're probably too old.

The meeting ended, the lights came up, and the auditorium began emptying. I joined the other Heritage members as they disassembled the sound system and packed it into our bus. I tried to forget the idea of running for Miss America, but the thought nagged me. I had felt that it was time for a change. Could this be it?

We finished packing the bus, ate supper, then went back to our motel. As I lay in bed that night, I tossed frequently, trying to keep the idea out of my mind. It looked like such a big challenge, and I loved challenges. Could I really do it?

"Lord," I finally prayed, "if You want me to run for this thing, please give me a sign. A *big* one! I don't want any questions in my mind."

Finally I dropped off to sleep. The next morning we left for the next town on our concert schedule. Weeks went by, then months. Gradually I forgot about Miss America and the sign I'd prayed for from God.

Several months later I sat in a California salon getting my hair cut. Don, my hairdresser, talked about reincarnation as he clipped my wet hair.

"I've had several out-of-body experiences," he informed me as he secured a section of wet hair to the top of my head with a hot pick clip. "I have to believe in reincarnation—I've felt so many times that I've lived in other centuries." He combed my bangs over my eyes and concentrated on cutting them straight.

In the mirror I watched as the door to the salon opened and a sophisticated woman came in. She sat in the waiting area and picked up a magazine.

"My next client," Don informed me. He pulled half the wet hair down from the clip and started combing it out. I watched as the woman put down her magazine and stared at me. Embarrassed, I tried not to look at her.

"Don, do you believe when people die they join a great spirit of energy, or do they just go directly into a new person?"

Don knew I was a Christian. We frequently discussed the differences between our beliefs.

Before Don could answer, the woman got out of her chair and walked over to us. She still stared at me. I wondered if she thought she knew me from somewhere. "She probably thinks I'm her daughter's best friend or something," I mumbled to myself.

The woman approached me without hesitation. "Excuse me." She stepped in front of my chair. "I'm with the Miss California Pageant board, and I've been watching you today. I really feel you should enter a pageant. I'll give you any amount of help I can." She stopped and looked a little puzzled. "I don't know what it is, but I just really felt I needed to tell you that."

I slumped in the chair, wide-eyed, and feeling like I'd been struck with a sack of bricks. I'd almost forgotten about praying for a sign.

"Thank you," I stammered. "I . . . I'll think about it."

She handed me her card. "Give me a call if you need my help." She turned and sat back down with her magazine.

Don stood aside and stared at me. "Well!" His voice trailed off.

I nodded my head, unable to answer. My mind whirled. I knew Miss California preliminaries were already over, but this had to be the sign I'd prayed for.

Questions raced through my mind. When did Idaho hold its preliminary competitions? Would I even be out of Heritage Singers in time? Would I be too old to run? I promised myself that as soon as I got home to Idaho, I'd find answers to every one of them.

I arrived home in Idaho and found most of the preliminary competitions had already taken place. I also discovered that because of my age I couldn't run the next year. I felt disappointed, yet relieved. "Perhaps that woman's comment was just coincidence," I told myself. "A very strange coincidence."

I got a regular job and started living a regular life until a small newspaper article disrupted everything. The article stated that all the preliminary girls had been chosen except Miss Treasure Valley. Miss Treasure Valley! That was my hometown preliminary!

Everything seemed too coincidental to ignore. I swallowed my fear and tried to forget everything I'd ever thought about pageant girls. I'd be different, I promised myself. I prayed as I filled out the application. "Lord, help me not to offend anyone with this. Help this to be the right thing to do. I don't want people to think I'm doing this for my glory. Help them to see You through me."

Chapter 2

Miss Treasure Valley

"And Miss Treasure Valley, 1989 is . . ." the announcer paused for effect as drums rolled, ". . . Rebecca Eileen Trueblood!"

I gasped as the former Miss Treasure Valley put a crown on my head. Blinking back tears, I accepted the congratulations of the other girls and waved to the audience. I walked the small stage, waving and smiling. My family cheered louder than the rest of the crowd.

After walking the stage, I stood in the center with the first and second runners-up while a camera flashed. My face hurt from smiling so much.

"I can't believe this is happening!" I breathed to myself as the photographer snapped another picture. "I never expected to win."

After the picture taking, a reporter from the local paper started asking questions. "Did you think you were going to win?" "How does it feel to know you'll be competing for Miss Idaho?" "What do you think you'll do during your year as Miss Treasure Valley?"

Each question seemed to come faster than the one before, and I answered them as well as I could. More questions. More pictures. The audience drifted away, till just the families of the winners remained. My family accepted the congratulations of some of the other parents. I couldn't wait to talk to them. Everyone else was so caught up in the pageant and its aftermath that my parents were the only ones I could talk to.

The photographer and reporter finally seemed to have enough and left. My Treasure Valley board members greeted me and gave me a list of dates and responsibilities. I suddenly had local appearances to make. Almost immediately I had to shop for glitter gowns and get sponsors to help me pay for the dresses. It all seemed to happen so quickly.

Well after midnight, the evening finally ended. My feet ached, my face hurt from smiling so much, but I felt great. I walked eagerly to where my parents waited. Wrapping my arms around them, I let the tears come.

My dad hugged me close. "I love you, honey."

Aunts, uncles, and grandparents crowded around, each one giving me a hug. I could feel the love and support in each hug and kiss. I felt so happy and so relieved to have worked hard and achieved what I'd wanted.

"You did so well, honey." Mom hugged me tightly. "I'm so proud of you."

I looked at my brother Todd. He'd been silent during this whole exchange. He smiled and put one arm around my waist. I knew he felt proud of me. Inside, I felt closer to him than I ever had.

We drove home together, talking over all the events of the evening and discussing what came next. But by the time we arrived home, all I wanted was to crawl in bed and sleep for at least twelve hours.

The next few weeks blurred past. I tried to prepare for the Miss Idaho contest, but work, appearances, and shopping trips seemed to crowd my days. I overheard people comparing me to Miss Boise, Melanie Jeanne Lavoie, and felt nervous. Melanie appeared confident and self-assured. She had won several preliminaries before, and seemed destined to win the Miss Idaho crown.

I knew that my travels with the Heritage Singers and my extensive stage experience would help me, but I didn't know if having more pageant experience would give her unspoken points with the judges.

Melanie and I did a few appearances together, and the more I got to know her, the more I admired her. We became good friends—something I hadn't expected from a competitor. At one appearance, the Boise Host Lions Club, I heard her sing for the first time.

"She's *good*," I thought as she finished her song. "She's really, *really* good."

I knew, as I watched her, that the things I'd heard were right. She would be very, very strong competition to me.

I also worried about becoming too involved in the pageant world. Everyone seemed to want me to change everything about myself. I'd accepted the Lord into my life at the age of four, and I'd always wanted my life to be something He could be proud of. Now so many people wanted me to compromise. I fought it, trying to stay natural.

"Lord," I prayed, "just let me use this to Your glory. Help me never to lose sight of who You want me to be."

The pageant loomed closer. I tried to fit exercise, the newspaper, and practicing my song into my schedule, but there never seemed to be enough time. As word of the Miss Idaho pageant spread to family and friends via word of mouth, I started getting letters and phone calls. I never seemed to have time to answer all of them. The guilt of ignoring my correspondence and the hectic schedule wore on me.

I clung to my family. As I had less and less time to devote to friends, my parents supported and loved me. I knew whatever happened, my family would be there for me.

One evening everything seemed to close in on me. No matter how much time I put into the pageant and my job, it never seemed to be enough. Everyone wanted more from me. Always a very private person, I tried to keep my frustrations to myself. I never wanted people to see me upset; I always wanted them to like me. When it became too much one day, I collapsed in a chair and poured everything out to my mother.

"There's so much preparation involved! I got up and exercised, read the paper, and practiced—all before putting in a full day's work! This can't be worth it."

Mom listened, not interrupting.

"And besides," I continued. "I want to be Miss Idaho, but I'm really afraid people will think I've gotten involved in this because I miss the glory of singing with Heritage." I thought of Melanie and how people compared the two of us. "Melanie's so good. I'm putting everything on the line for this pageant. I'm scared of not coming up good. What if my best isn't good enough?"

"Why do you think you're trying for the title?" Mom asked quietly.

"I don't know anymore!" Calming, I smiled slightly. "Actually, I *do* know. I'm doing it because I love a challenge and because I really feel God wants me to do this." I frowned. "It seems like such a contradiction though."

Again Mom waited for me to continue.

"Everything in the pageant world seems to go against Christian values. They want me to fit into their mold." I sarcastically flicked my long hair. "If my hair isn't right, the system changes it. If my nails aren't right, the system changes them. People want me to have an air about myself."

"The Becki I know has never backed down under pressure before," Mom reminded me. "You'll weather this too."

"Yeah, I suppose so," I agreed. "But is the prize worth going through the pressure?"

"Only you can decide that," Mom replied. "You know that we'll be proud of you no matter what you do. We've always prayed you'd make the right decisions with your life. I know you have too."

I smiled, feeling less tense.

"You've prayed for God's guidance. Now you must believe He is leading in your life." Mom walked over and hugged me.

"I know." I hugged her back.

Over the next few days I kept remembering my mother's words. God *did* want me here. I sang the words to one of my Heritage solos, "Best for Me," over and over in my mind. And no matter what happened at the Miss Idaho competition, I knew God was in control.

Some dreams refused to die though. Every time I reached out to a young school child or spoke to a small business in Caldwell, a thought kept repeating.

"You could be reaching more people," I reminded myself. "As Miss Idaho, and then as Miss America, God can use you to reach many, many more people just the way you're reaching people in your hometown now." The dream pushed me in spite of my exhaustion.

Two weeks until the pageant.

One week.

I studied my interview notes carefully and practiced my solo until I was sick of it.

Six days.

Five days.

I exercised more, tanned daily.

Four days.

Three days.

Through everything I prayed constantly.

"You know you'll at least place," I tried to console myself. "Your travels and stage experience give you a little edge."

The positive thinking helped, but not much. I figured

that normally I'd do better in every area of competition, but right now I was less than my best because of my exhausting work schedule.

Two days.

One day.

My gown for the evening gown competition, my talent gown, the interview outfit—all hung pressed, dry-cleaned, and ready for the trip to Boise. Suitcases overflowed with daily clothes, dresses for appearances. I nervously checked details like nylons and makeup. I slept little and prayed a lot.

Four hours.

Three hours.

I went through the preparation and trip to Boise almost in a fog. My mother drove and kept the conversation running smoothly in the car. I answered her mindlessly. The familiar Idaho landscape seemed foreign today, and the usually short drive from Caldwell to Boise took forever. I couldn't believe it was happening.

"And Lord, You know what's best for me. You want what's best for me." The words to the song I'd sung so long ago comforted me. I felt my fear depart and a new determination take its place.

"I'll make it through this," I promised myself. "I'll do my very best, and I'll make it through this."

Chapter 3

The Other Girls

The whirlwind week of activity started as soon as we arrived at the hotel. The mayor of Boise greeted each of the contestants individually. I met my hostess and some of the other contestants.

"All this attention makes me feel a little uncomfortable," I told my pageant companion as we rode the elevator up to our rooms.

"Get used to it," she replied. "It's much bigger at the Miss America contest."

I laughed and followed her out of the elevator, down the hall, and into the room. My roommate, Miss Idaho Falls, had already arrived. She turned from the closet to greet me.

"Hi!" she bubbled. "I'm Darady. You must be Rebecca."

"Yes," I replied. "You can call me Becki. Rebecca's my pageant name." I smiled at her. "How long have you been here?"

"I only got in about an hour ago." She turned to me, her eyes dancing. "Isn't this the most exciting thing of your life?"

Her enthusiasm matched mine, and we chatted nonstop. I asked about her preliminary pageant, she asked about mine. And as we headed for supper, I determined to make this the most fun week I could.

"I may be in competition with these girls," I told myself, "but there's no reason why I can't be their friend."

At supper that night I carefully watched the other girls. They all seemed so poised and self-assured. I saw Melanie coming across the room toward me, and I smiled in greeting.

"Hi!" we said at the same time, then laughed.

"Can you believe the pageant is finally here?" I asked her as we sat down at a table.

"I know," she agreed. "It seems like we've been waiting forever for this!"

As we began eating, I looked at Melanie, Darady, and the other contestants. Everyone laughed and chatted easily with each other. I'd always heard that pageants were full of catty, back-stabbing contestants. Everyone here seemed so nice. After supper, I worked my way around the room and met all the other girls. Looking at each contestant, I wondered how the judges could ever make their choice. Each one looked destined to wear the crown.

Each of us received our itineraries for the week, then returned to our rooms. I looked at mine and sighed. It seemed like every minute of the week had some obligation.

The activities began early the next morning with practice for the final night. After practice came public appearances. Each day followed the same pattern. One afternoon we went to Boise's mall, another, we visited the capitol. None of it seemed like serious competition until Thursday.

Thursday. After three days of fun and extremely hard work, the real competition began. First there were interviews. I'd prepared as best I could by reading the paper, taking notes, and memorizing. I felt, however, that I didn't have the time to really do my best. Practice seemed quieter than usual. Each of us became a little more reserved. The camaraderie that had marked the first part of the week faded, and I felt a little strained. The competition had begun.

After rehearsing the opening number, I sat down on the stage next to Melanie. She looked thoughtful.

"This is the last year I'm doing this," she informed me. "In fact, my parents are flying out from Massachusetts for the final night." She turned and smiled at me, her serious mood gone. "You all ready for your interview this afternoon?"

"Yeah, sure," I replied brightly. But I watched her quietly. What if *I* had tried for so many years to become Miss Idaho? How would I feel if *my* parents traveled a long distance to see me win, and I lost? What if this was *my* last chance to try for something I wanted so badly? Once again I admired Melanie for being so friendly to me and the other girls.

After practice, I changed into my interview suit and went over my notes. Being number fifteen, the last girl, I worried. Would being last hurt or help me? I alternately studied my facts and prayed. I prayed for wisdom, poise, and most of all, energy. The week's activities had drained me of what little I had had when I'd arrived.

As I entered the interview room I put on an air of confidence I didn't feel deep inside. "You have seven minutes to convince them you're the next Miss Idaho," I silently reminded myself, smiling broadly.

The judges smiled back at me, looking a little tired. I sat in my chair and waited for the questions to start. A gray-haired man picked up some papers and studied them quickly.

"You appear to have traveled quite extensively with the Heritage Singers," he began. "What was your favorite country, and why?"

I relaxed instantly. Traveling with Heritage was something I could talk about for hours. The open-ended questions about Heritage continued. I smiled and responded animatedly. This was fun!

The interview ended with one current event question. I left the room feeling great. As I went over all the questions in my mind and reviewed my answers, I knew I'd done the very best I could have.

Friday. The reserve I sensed in the other girls the day before seemed even more pronounced today. I sat and listened to the other girls rehearse their talent numbers. Everyone seemed so good, and I could feel a knot of nervousness inside. I felt I had a good chance of making the top eight, but my confidence of winning the Miss Idaho crown went down. I knew the other girls probably felt as nervous as I did. We all knew that tonight's preliminary competition would decide the top eight contestants.

I worked through my rehearsal carefully. I really wanted more time to get used to the stage and sound system. It didn't sound quite right, and I felt really nervous. I felt happy with the song I'd chosen, and I loved my dress, but the sound system made me nervous. After practice, all I could do was wait, and that was the hardest part.

I knew I would see my parents that afternoon at a luncheon for the girls and their parents. I couldn't wait to see my family. It had only been a few days, but home seemed like a lifetime away. The pageant had taken all my focus and energy.

After rehearsal and a quick clothes change, the other girls and I arrived at the luncheon. The large room was filled with nervous-looking parents. I scanned the room quickly for my family. For one quick second I feared they hadn't arrived yet, but then I spotted them in the far left-hand corner. I walked quickly toward them, trying not to run. They silently opened their arms for me, and I started crying as they hugged me close. No one spoke for a few minutes.

"I've really missed you guys," I said as I dried my tears.

"How are you doing?" Mom asked. "Did your interview go well? Are you getting enough rest?"

"I think so," I replied. I looked at my parents—two sane, normal, loving people in the middle of all the pageant hype. My eyes welled up again, and I hugged them tightly.

"We're here for you, no matter what," Mom spoke gently. "We'll be proud of you whether you win or don't."

The luncheon passed too quickly. I sat very close to my parents, touching them often.

"We'll be praying and cheering for you tonight," Mom promised.

I left them, reluctantly, to prepare for the preliminary competition. The dressing room was unusually quiet as each girl carefully applied makeup and donned glittery gowns.

"This is it," I thought to myself as I finished putting on my eye makeup. "Oh, Lord, be with me."

The competition began. The excitement of the evening caught all the contestants. I sang, interviewed, and modeled my way through the various competitions, and returned to sit with the other contestants. As the evening ended, we eyed each other carefully. The judges had made their decisions. We knew we wouldn't find out who had made the list until the next night, but we knew the top eight had been chosen.

After the preliminaries, the pageant hosted a banquet for the contestants. Candlelight highlighted the beautiful gowns and flawless faces. All the girls talked, relieved to be done with the preliminary competition. We decided to have a private party for the winner after the final night.

That night in bed, I tried to guess who the top eight would be. I guessed Melanie would make the list, and I hoped I would, and I also thought my roommate, Darady, would be included. It irritated me not to know for sure.

"Why can't they do the preliminaries and finals on the same night?" I muttered to myself as I tried to find a comfortable position. Sleep eluded me.

The final day. The big final competition. We all felt nervous and a little giddy. I knew that a new Miss Idaho would be crowned that night, and I wanted it to be me. Looking at the other girls' faces, I knew they all felt the same way.

That morning we did all the television taping, and in the afternoon we did a full dress rehearsal. After the rehearsal, we were given time to relax and prepare for the pageant. A table of food had been set up, but we barely touched it.

"I can't believe all this great food is sitting around, and I'm not touching a bite!" joked two other girls.

"We'll have pizza tonight after the pageant," one of the girls said, grinning.

A few hours before the pageant, we began getting ready. It seemed like a more serious repeat of the night before. As I put the finishing touches on my hair, I looked at the other girls. Excitement glittered in each pair of eyes. Grim determination lined each mouth. Melanie caught my gaze and smiled confidently. I turned back to my own reflection in the mirror. My eyes shone with the same excitement I'd seen in the other girls' eyes.

"Oh, Lord, help me keep my focus on You," I prayed silently as I sprayed my hair. "It's so easy to get caught up in all this stuff."

I carefully applied makeup, smoothing on just enough to appear natural under the hot lights. With each stroke of the makeup brush I watched the every-day Becki disappear and a glamorous Becki take her place. Inside I knew the real me never disappeared. Only the outside changed.

"Oh, Lord, help me never to forget who I am inside," I prayed. "Give me Your peace. Help me remember I am Your child." "And . . . You know what's best for me."

The phrase comforted me again. I felt the last of my fear drain away. God had put me in this contest, and He *did* know what was best for me. I stared at my reflection. "You're still the same old Becki," I reminded myself, grinning.

A pageant official poked her head in the room. "Fifteen minutes, ladies."

I stepped into my dress and high heels. The mirror reflected a confident, smiling girl. I checked for any makeup mistakes, any runs in my nylons.

"Five minutes!"

The other girls and I looked at each other. I realized this was the last time we'd all be on the same level. Before the night ended, one of us would be Miss Idaho.

The official came back and led us to the side of the stage where we waited for our cue. My hands felt damp with excitement.

"Let's go get 'um!" someone in front of me whispered. "Let's go get 'um!"

Chapter **4**

Miss Idaho 1989

Music pulsated from large speakers as we took our places on stage for the first number. We had barely reached our spots when the curtain opened and we danced, sang, and smiled in time with the music. I tried to see where my family sat, but the bright spotlights made it impossible to see beyond the end of the stage. Except for the sound of cheering, we could have been rehearsing again.

I glanced at the other contestants as we moved in our carefully choreographed steps. The swirl of black-and-white dresses blended with the bright lights and brilliant smiles.

"This is for real," I thought as I felt my excitement rise.

The first number ended perfectly, and we stood frozen in our places as Miss Idaho 1988 walked the stage. The evening's hostess, Patricia Tauzin of Texas, first runner-up to Miss America the year before, gave some opening remarks. I concentrated on smiling and remembering what to say when I had to introduce myself.

"And now we want you to meet your contestants for the 1989 Miss Idaho crown," the hostess said.

Melanie stepped confidently to the mike and introduced herself. Miss Eastern Idaho followed. Miss Twin Falls. The fourteen contestants before me ran through their introductions quickly. I smiled and walked confidently to the mike.

"I'm Miss Treasure Valley, Rebecca Eileen Trueblood."

Loud cheering erupted from the left side of the auditorium, and now I knew where my family was seated. Smiling and waving, I walked the small runway and stepped back into place with the other girls.

Miss Idaho 1988 came back on stage. She looked so comfortable wearing the crown. I wondered if she felt glad to be through with her year or if she wished she could be Miss Idaho again.

"Tonight's judging will be based on talent, 40 percent; interview, 30 percent; swimsuit and evening gown, 15 percent each. And now for the eight semi-finalists!"

The hostess paused for effect, and I gritted my teeth. "Why draw this out," I wondered.

"Miss Boise, Melanie Jeanne Lavoie!"

The crowd erupted in applause. My hands felt damp again, but this time with nervousness.

"Miss Eastern Idaho, Stephanie Anne Smith."

More applause, more sweaty palms.

"Miss Meridian, Pamela Westover!"

"Miss Idaho National Guard, Amy Lyn Kendell!"

I didn't hear the next few finalists, and I gritted my teeth, smiled, and prayed.

"Miss Treasure Valley, Rebecca Eileen Trueblood!"

I didn't hear the last part of my name because of the cheering that came from my family's section of the audience. I joined the other semifinalists, and we smiled, stepped back, and watched the curtain fall.

The instant the curtain was in place, pandemonium broke out backstage. The other seven semifinalists and I raced to the dressing room, ripped off our dresses, and put on swimsuits.

"Anybody got hairspray?" one of the semifinalists cried. "I ran out!"

Three cans of the precious liquid made their way to the girl's hand.

I stood in front of the mirror, turning from side to side. As I examined my reflection, I remembered being a chubby kid and getting teased about rolls on my stomach. I knew my hours of exercise had me toned and fit, but I couldn't help feeling afraid.

"Come on, girls, you're on!"

We rushed back to the stage, where the hostess was just finishing a ventriloquist act. We composed ourselves through a commercial break and felt ready to go back on stage as the hostess announced the swimsuit competition.

I watched Melanie leave first. She looked toned, tanned, and utterly confident in her pink swimsuit. I nervously waited my turn after the other contestants. Finally, I stepped on stage and into the bright lights again.

I slowly, carefully walked the stage, turning in the right places and smiling. The hostess talked about my career goals and my experiences with Heritage. After doing one more turn, I walked off stage and breathed again.

"Five minutes until talent!"

I raced back to the dressing room and quickly put my long, glittery blue dress on. The first contestants were already on their way to the stage as I began repairing my makeup and hair. Trying to warm my voice up, I hummed through the song as I finished getting ready.

"I'm changing from what I was before . . ."

The words of Michael O'Brien's song reminded me, once again, of who I was and why I was here. I remembered how I'd searched everywhere for just the right song. I wanted a crossover song—one that could be either a love song or a religious one. As soon as I heard "Changing," I knew it was the one. I felt determined to reach at least one person in the audience that night with my song.

I walked backstage and paced, praying, as I waited for my turn. As I listened to the other talent numbers, I heard some of the girls who had finished say they had not done as well as in the preliminaries. It made me nervous.

"Lord, help me not to forget the words to my song," I breathed. "Help me to sing for You." Inside I felt peace in knowing so many people were praying for me.

After hearing my name announced, I walked on stage and smiled as I waited for my tape to start. The reassuringly familiar music washed over me, and I poured myself into the song and its message. The peace I had felt before I started stayed with me, and I knew I was reaching the audience. I felt great as I finished the song and walked backstage. I didn't care whether the judges liked me or not.

The evening gown competition. Another quick dress change. I rushed to the dressing room, quickly changed my dress, and ran back to the stage. As I got backstage I noticed a run in my nylons. Frantically I signaled to my traveling companion. "I've got a run in my nylons! Can you get me another pair?"

She nodded and ran back to the dressing room. Three minutes later she returned, hose in hand.

"Here." She thrust the nylons at me as she gasped for air. "Change in the food area—it's closer."

I ripped off the ruined nylons with one hand and rushed to put on the next pair. I could hear the commercial ending and the next number being announced as I ran out of the food area and onto the stage. The curtain rose as I ran across the stage. Reaching my spot, I slid and fell into another girl. I could hear snickers from the audience.

". . . and starting our evening gown competition this evening, Miss Boise, Melanie Jean Lavoie . . ."

Melanie walked to the stage and modeled the gown

as Patricia told the audience Melanie's height, hair color, and eye color. I tried to compose myself and catch my breath. Miss Eastern Idaho followed, then Miss Meridian. With a bit of surprise I realized this would be the last competition of the evening. Soon one of us would be Miss Idaho.

I walked the stage carefully and listened to the hostess announce my physical characteristics. Walking to the center of the stage, I joined the other eight semifinalists as the audience applauded all of us. We walked backstage, where all the other contestants had their gowns on for the final number.

During commercial break the hostess did another ventriloquist act. All the former Miss Idahos, here for the fortieth celebration, greeted the audience. Miss Idaho 1988 did her farewell walk. Another commercial break. I felt like we stood and waited forever. Finally, we all walked back on stage. The finalists stood on one side, the nonfinalists on the other. The other finalists and I stood holding hands.

"A civic award from Fruit of the Loom goes to Miss Idaho National Guard, Amy Lyn Kendell!"

Amy broke her grip on the rest of us and accepted her award. My right hand, which gripped the hand of another contestant, felt damp. Silently, smiling, we watched as the judges handed the hostess the list of winners.

"And now for the moment we've all been waiting for." The hostess paused. The fourth runner-up, and the winner of a five-hundred-and-fifty-dollar scholarship, is Miss Idaho Falls, Darady Sommers!"

The audience broke into applause as the fourth runner-up took her place in the winners' lineup.

"The third runner-up, and the winner of a six-hundred-and-fifty-dollar scholarship, is Miss Idaho National Guard, Amy Lyn Kendell!"

More applause. The other semifinalists and I grasped

hands tighter. I looked at Melanie. She looked as nervous as I felt.

"The second runner-up is Miss Rexburg Upper Valley, Rama Jean Griffith!"

The remaining girls and I gripped each other's hands. It felt like a live electrical current running through all of us and our connecting hands.

"The role of the first runner-up is very important," the hostess informed the audience. "If for any reason Miss Idaho cannot perform her duties, the first runner-up must take her place." She paused and looked at the card in her hand.

The audience went quiet, waiting.

"The first runner-up, and the winner of a one-thousand-dollar scholarship, is Miss Boise, Melanie Jean Lavoie.

Melanie broke from the rest of us and went forward to receive her prize. She smiled, but I could see tears forming behind her perfect façade.

"Miss Idaho, 1989 is . . . may I have a drum roll please."

I looked at the other runners-up and thought, "Oh my goodness, can it be me?"

"Miss Treasure Valley, Rebecca Eileen Trueblood."

Loud whooping and cheering accompanied the announcement. I put my hands to my face, shocked, and blinked back tears. I hugged the girl next to me. Someone put the banner on me, and Miss Idaho 1988 crowned me. Flowers appeared in my arms.

I began my walk around the stage and down the small runway. Holding the flowers in one hand, I alternately waved and wiped the tears from my face with the other.

"I can't believe it, I just can't believe it! This has got to be a dream!" The thought kept turning over and over in my mind as I finished my walk and stood on the winner's platform. All the runners-up stood around me.

Cameras flashed, and Claudia Weathermon, the news anchor from Channel 6, started asking me questions.

"How does it feel to have won Miss Idaho?" she asked, thrusting the microphone my direction.

"I don't think there are words to express how this feels." My voice shook a little, and I stopped to get control of myself. "On TV you see the Miss Americas, how they break out crying. Believe me, it's not a joke. It really happens. I'm so excited. Thank you so much, judges. Thank you!"

Audience applause followed my last thank you. The reporter smiled and began asking another question. "Are you prepared for the changes that will happen this year?"

"I don't really know what's ahead, but I'm very excited for the challenge," I replied. "I promise to do my very best."

The questions continued. I answered with a sense of unreality. "This can't be happening," I thought. "It just can't be real."

All of the Miss Idaho winners from previous years attended this pageant, and Miss Barbara Norton Brown, Miss Idaho 1950, came back on stage to congratulate me. Stepping to the mike, she smiled my direction before speaking.

"Nothing can replace a genuine love and caring," she said, "and I think you'll be a knockout back East."

The audience went wild again, and I mouthed a thank you to her.

Claudia decided to ask more questions. "What did you think of the competition?" she asked.

"It was extremely tough," I answered honestly. "From the very beginning everyone was *so good!* I have to say that every one of these girls deserves to wear this crown as much as I do."

The reporter looked at me and the runners-up. "I see

a lot of tears here," she teased.

Darady wiped back her tears and smiled. "I'm just so glad Becki won," she blurted.

Claudia congratulated us all again and signed off with the station. Photographers, reporters, and the other contestants swarmed around me. Instantly I found myself the center of what felt like undeserved attention. It seemed like everyone wanted part of me. Gradually everyone moved to where the pageant officials had set up a party in my honor.

My family was waiting for me. I cried as I walked toward them. My dad held me as I cried. "I can't believe it," I exclaimed. "It all seems like such a dream."

The reporters kept asking me questions. The pageant officials presented me with a fur coat, a car, and other prizes. I couldn't remember when I'd ever been so happy.

"How do you feel about competing in the Miss America Pageant this September?" one of the reporters asked me.

I stopped short. I'd almost forgotten I'd be going to Atlantic City. "I can't wait," I replied enthusiastically.

The rest of the night whirled by. It seemed like I hugged, kissed, and talked to more people than I had ever known. Inside I felt so happy. Nothing could pull me down. I didn't feel I'd ever need to sleep or eat again.

And above all, I felt at peace. The craziness of the party around me couldn't touch the deep inner peace I had inside. "Lord," I whispered. "I know I'm right at the center of where You want me to be. Thank You."

I felt that all of my life had been a preparation for this. All the experiences I'd had growing up, all the rough times in my life, everything led up to this moment. And I wondered, as I looked forward to the challenge of Atlantic City, could God want me to be the next Miss America?

The party ended after midnight. The pageant officials escorted me back to the hotel where all the other girls waited for me. As I stepped off the elevator onto our hall, my fellow contestants applauded. I blinked back tears.

"So, did you guys save me any pizza?" I asked, trying to lighten the mood.

"You bet," Darady replied. "And lots of candy too!"

I grabbed a handful of chocolates and sat on the floor next to everyone else. Darady handed me a piece of pizza.

"Real food at last," I joked. "I've been waiting for this!"

I looked at the girls. They were all laughing and joking with one another, all except Melanie. I leaned over to Darady.

"Where's Melanie?" I asked quietly.

"Um . . . I think she went to dinner with her parents."

Two other girls, overhearing us, exchanged knowing looks. I could tell they thought Melanie had skipped the party for other reasons.

The party went on until, exhausted and stuffed, the girls excused themselves one by one and returned to their rooms. I waited for Melanie. Somehow I knew she wasn't angry. Just extremely disappointed. About two-thirty in the morning, she got off the elevator.

"Hi, Melanie," I said quietly.

She looked at me and tried to smile. I could see tear stains still fresh on her cheeks. "Sorry I missed the party," she said weakly.

I stood up and put my hand on her arm. She started crying.

"Let's go talk," I suggested.

We sat on the floor in the hall as she tried to stop her tears.

"Becki, you must believe me when I say that I'm happy for you," she cried. "It's just that I wanted to be Miss Idaho so badly . . ." her voice trailed off.

I could feel my own tears forming. I knew how hard she'd worked for this, how much she wanted it. I'd worked just as hard, and wanted it just as badly. And I knew how I'd feel if our situations were reversed.

"I know, I know," I replied, tears flowing down my face.

We sat silently crying together, our hands touching. I wished I could say something to make her feel better, but somehow I knew that nothing I might do or say could take away the pain.

Chapter 5

The Making of a Pageant Winner

Winning the biggest scholarship pageant in the United States takes much, much more than a pretty smile and perfect figure. Before entering a pageant myself, I'd never dreamed of all the hard work every contestant must put in to be ready for Atlantic City.

Immediately after winning Miss Idaho, my life focused solely on the Miss America Pageant. On a typical day I dragged myself out of bed at 6:00 a.m. and ran for half an hour. After that I watched "Good Morning America" for two hours, during which I did floor exercises. For the rest of the morning I read *USA Today* and the *The Idaho Statesman* in detail. To remember everything, I kept a notebook complete with indexes and subjects.

After eating and showering, I met with my interview coach. Later I either met with my vocal coach or one of the board members. This took all afternoon. In the evenings I made appearances at other pageants, looked for sponsors, or did stuff for existing sponsors. Finally, at 10:30 p.m., I came back home and exercised my way through "Entertainment Tonight" and "Nightline," and finished my evening with "Arsenio Hall" just for fun.

Everything I had, everything I was, went into preparing for the pageant. All areas of my life came under attack. I had a group of people governing me who always seemed to have different ideas of how I should be. I tried to keep everyone happy yet stay focused at the same time.

"Lord, I don't know what I should do to prepare for this," I prayed often. "Help me to choose the right song, the right clothes. Help me to spend my time and money wisely."

Letters and phone calls started pouring in from all over the world. Everyone had a similar message! "Becki, I don't know what it is, but I just feel God has something really special for you."

Each letter and call reminded me again that God had called me to this. Every time I got tired or frustrated, I remembered the encouragement of my friends, prayed for strength, and pushed myself harder.

My hectic schedule forced me to ignore many of my friends. I simply didn't have time to devote to them. They, in turn, couldn't understand what I was experiencing.

"This thing is taking over my whole life," I complained to my closest friends many times. "It has to be my focus. It's the hardest thing I've ever done."

"It really must be tough," one commiserated. "I'll be here for you."

But each time I talked to them, I knew they wondered how something like a pageant could consume so much of me. My family understood, and I found, as the summer wore on, that they were the only ones I had to count on.

"Mom," I cried one evening, "it's just so hard to know what's right. Every day I make decisions that will affect the outcome in Atlantic City. How do I know what's right?"

"Becki," she reminded me. "You know that when you accept God's will in your life, He will give you the desires of your heart. You've prayed sincerely and honestly for His will. We've all prayed for His will. God will guide your decisions."

"I know, Mom," I agreed. "This isn't easy, though."

"Whoever said God's will is easy?"

The summer wore on. I kept working. Every day I exercised just a little bit more, made myself jog a half mile farther, did extra sit-ups. I tanned and toned myself into a magazine's ideal of the perfect body.

A woman out of Idaho Falls taught me to walk correctly. My board members taught me to speak correctly. Daily shopping trips brought more changes. They wanted me to dress like a pageant winner. I wanted to dress a little more conservatively. Every step, mannerism, facial expression, and tone of my voice was open to correction.

My interview coach, Fred Horman, drilled me daily about world events. We went over and over every detail until I felt I knew enough about politics and issues to run a small country. Still, we kept working.

My vocal coach worked on perfecting my voice. Of all the areas of my life, this was the hardest to take correction in. I'd been singing since I was six years old, and I'd had five years experience with the Heritage Singers, yet now someone was telling me that the things I had thought I did well, I could do better. She showed me how.

Bit by bit I saw myself being broken down. Nothing I'd been before was good enough. Doing my best and pleasing these people became my life. And because they were the only people around me, except for my family, they defined my life.

The summer had its fun times too, though. I did an appearance at the Washington pageant and watched the crowning of a new Miss Washington. I visited schools and talked to business people. Children listened to me talk and sing, their eyes shining with their own dreams. Everywhere I went, I spoke the same message:

"If you want to be or do something badly, you have to work for it; and if you work hard and long enough, you will achieve your goal."

I believed my message. I knew the hard work I put into preparing for the Miss America Pageant would be worth it.

Over the rest of the summer I learned the dos and don'ts of being a titleholder. Every time I left my house, even if I just wanted to shop or go out to eat, I had to be "appropriately dressed." My board members defined this as looking respectable. Perfect lipstick, flawless nails, and salon-styled hair completed the picture.

"Remember, Becki, you're representing an entire state of people and the Miss Idaho Pageant," they reminded me. "People expect their Miss Idaho to be beautiful and perfect. And it's good practice for when you become Miss America."

As the Miss America Pageant drew closer, the letters, cards, and phone calls became more and more frequent. People from Idaho wrote telling me they were sure I'd be the next Miss America. Everyone encouraged me. I felt overwhelmed by the confidence everyone seemed to have in me.

"I can't believe it's possible that I might be Miss America," I said to my interview coach one afternoon. I'd been saying that to him all summer.

He looked very seriously into my face. "Becki, I don't want you to ever say it's 'possible.' You want to be Miss America. You must believe it."

I looked at him, a little taken aback. "That sounds so . . . so presumptuous."

"Believe it," he instructed me. "You've worked hard. You can win. Every time you doubt, I want you to imagine the announcers calling your name as Miss America. OK?"

I agreed, but inside I doubted him a little.

Yet over the rest of the summer, my own confidence

grew, and my doubts fled. A few weeks before the pageant, I felt I was at my very best in all areas of my life. I felt physically fit, I could speak for hours on world events, and my vocal number stretched me as a performer. I felt ready. I couldn't wait to get back to Atlantic City and take on my next challenge.

My family lived every up and down of the summer with me. For the entire time, my pageant became the focus of the family.

"We're proud of you," Dad told me.

"We've never had any doubts that if you got close enough you could take the crown," Mom said. "We've prayed and worked hard for this. Now we have to believe it will all turn out as it should."

I listened and believed. From my very first memories I'd been told that if two or three people pray together, God will answer their prayers. I knew people all over the world prayed for me, and I believed God would respond to those prayers.

I also prayed that if I didn't make Miss America, God would help me handle it. But I felt that with all the people I had praying for me, together with my own hard work and the signs that had led me into the pageant world, I was destined for the Miss America crown.

Chapter 6

Down Home
With Becki

"Can we get a shot of you and Skip together?"

I smiled obligingly at the photographer and posed with Skip Smyser, a state representative. Many government people and businessmen had shown up for my going-away party. I obediently posed and smiled for pictures with each one.

I looked around the Trolley Square reception hall, amazed. My Treasure Valley board seemed intent on giving me a going-away party I'd never forget.

"If I could have everyone's attention, please . . ."

I turned and faced a small stage area where the director of the Treasure Valley board stood. He smiled as everyone quit talking and waited for him to continue.

"I want to thank every one of you for being here tonight to honor Becki. We have a great evening planned, and we're pleased you're here to give Becki the send-off she deserves!"

Applause followed his last words. I blushed slightly and looked around the room. My board members had really tried to set up a first-class party. Coffee cake, hors d'œuvres, sandwiches, and punch graced a table in the corner. Town officials, board members, and business sponsors of "Down Home With Becki" milled around, greeting each other.

After the applause quieted, the announcer continued. "And now if we could get a few words from our honored guest . . ." He paused and smiled at me. "Becki, why don't you come up here and say hello."

I walked to the microphone, thanked the announcer, and turned to the audience. "Thank you all so much. This . . . this is incredible." I looked around the lavishly decorated room again. "I'm sure no girl has ever had such a great send-off! I'm so flattered that you care so much. Thank you, each of you, for this." I looked at my board members and smiled. "You've each done so much for me. I can't thank you enough."

I kept talking, till I looked out of the corner of my eye and saw the announcer patiently waiting to get the microphone back.

"You have to wait your turn, Becki," he teased. "I still have a few announcements to make."

I blushed and laughed. If he hadn't interrupted me, I knew I'd have kept talking all night. I couldn't help myself. I felt so shocked that people were so interested in me—that they cared so much.

The announcements ended. I circulated around the room and talked to as many people as possible. All the conversation centered on the Miss America Pageant.

"So, Becki, do you feel ready?" a woman across the table asked.

"As ready as I can be," I replied. "I've worked very hard for this. Of course I always wish I could do more, but I still feel ready."

"What area do you feel strongest in?" another woman asked.

"That's a hard one!" I answered. I stopped and thought a minute. "I guess I'd have to say talent only because I've been doing that the longest. I feel my experience with Heritage, and all my work before and after that, has given me extra confidence."

"Do you find the swimsuit competition degrading?" another woman asked.

"Quite the contrary," I replied honestly. "I feel part of being a whole, healthy person includes being fit. The swimsuit competition is a physical fitness competition, and because it's only 15 percent of the score, I think of this competition as a scholarship pageant."

I smiled at my board members, and they nodded in support. They had heard me answer this question before and had confidence I could handle it.

The dinner ended, and we piled into antique cars for a parade to Simplot Stadium. From my position of honor at the end of the line, I waved to people on the street. They waved and cheered back. Some gave me a "thumbs up" sign. I looked at the cars weaving through the traffic ahead of me and the people on the street and wondered how many would actually show up for the program in the stadium.

"How many people are they expecting?" I asked my driver.

"Oh, a couple hundred, I think," he replied.

Fifteen hundred people waited for us at Simplot Stadium! I gasped, overwhelmed by the enormity of the crowd.

"So many people . . ." I murmured to one of my Treasure Valley board members.

She smiled gently at me. "You've won their hearts, Becki, and they're here to wish you luck."

I looked at the sea of faces. Some looked familiar, most didn't. A sense of unreality came over me. I watched TV people setting up equipment, sound people doing last-minute checks, and I looked at the crowd again. I couldn't believe all these people had shown up just for me.

The evening's entertainment began with a local band. I sat with a few businessmen and Pete Cowles, the mayor of Caldwell, on the side of the stage. The crowd enthusiastically clapped to the band's rhythm.

After the band finished the song, Pete got up to speak. "I want to thank all of you for being here for 'Down Home With Becki.' We're proud of our girl and want to give her a real Idaho send-off!"

The crowd cheered.

"Becki, come on over here and say hello to all these folks!"

I stood and joined him in the center of the stage. The crowd still applauded as I took the microphone.

"I . . . I don't know what to say. Thank you all so much for your support. It will mean so much to me when I fly back to Atlantic City. I'll be taking each of you with me in my heart. Thank you."

The crowd cheered louder. Pete tipped the microphone his direction.

"I'll bet if we applaud really loudly we can get Becki to sing for us!"

The audience responded immediately. I hid a grin. He made everything sound so spontaneous. We'd carefully planned how many songs I'd sing weeks before. Graciously I accepted the microphone from him again and waited for the accompaniment to start.

The crowd grew silent as I started to sing. I felt my heart overflowing with love for these people. Beside me stood important people who had taken time out of their frantic schedules to be at this party. In front of me sat my friends and neighbors—people who all along had believed in and encouraged me.

As I finished the song, the crowd exploded with applause. I voiced a quiet thank-you into the mike before handing it to the next speaker. I stood aside again and listened to a short talk by an area legislator. Another musical group got up and performed. I found myself called back to the microphone by the evening's emcee.

"Becki, I'm sure there are lots of things you'd like to say to everyone here tonight. Some of us are lucky enough to know you, but some of the people here have never met you. Why don't you tell us a little about yourself?"

He handed me the microphone, and I turned to the audience with a smile. "I'm so excited to be your Miss Idaho . . ."

Applause drowned out the rest of my sentence. I laughed and tried again.

"I'm excited to be Miss Idaho because it gives me the opportunity to meet and share a part of myself with so many people. I love telling people, especially children, that they can be anything they want to be if they work hard enough. I want to use my position as Miss Idaho—and hopefully, Miss America—to encourage people. I want to be a positive influence."

I paused as the crowd applauded again. The emcee came forward with his own mike.

"Tell us what you're looking forward to most back at Atlantic City."

"Oh, everything!" I replied. After the laughter quieted, I continued. "Actually, I'm looking forward to singing on that big stage."

"Talking about performing, will you sing for us again?"

I agreed and sang another song. As I finished, the emcee joined me again.

"Don't you think she'll make us proud back in Atlantic City?" he asked.

The crowd cheered wildly. The emcee turned to me, and someone from backstage brought out a bouquet of roses. "These are for you, Becki."

The emcee handed me the roses. "Our prayers and love go back to Atlantic City with you."

I waved to the audience and, a little tearfully, said thank you again. The perfect red roses cascaded over my arm, and I inhaled their scent deeply.

"At this time we want to give each of you the chance to greet Becki personally. Let's give her a real Idaho send-off!"

I walked to where the stage hands had set a small platform. After handing my roses to someone, I stood with a tuxedoed escort and greeted the long lines of people. Everyone radiated so much love and encouragement. People pressed cards and gifts into my hands. An hour passed. I knew the party had been scheduled to end already, but people kept coming by to greet me. I shook hands, hugged, and kissed all of them.

"We're proud of you."

"You're going to knock them dead back East."

"We're praying for you."

Each word of encouragement, each hug, made me realize I wasn't going back to Atlantic City as just Becki. I was taking all these people back with me. I wanted to show them they were something. I wanted to show the world what wonderful people Idaho has. I wanted to win for *them*. Their belief in me strengthened my resolve to bring *them* the crown.

The steady stream of people turned to a trickle, then finally stopped. I descended the platform and joined the local news team to do the late news. "We're here at Simplot Stadium with Miss Idaho 1989, Rebecca Eileen Trueblood."

I smiled into the camera as TV weatherman Ron Watson's smooth voice continued. "Tell us, Becki, do you feel ready for the challenge of the Miss America competition?"

"I feel very ready," I replied. "So many people have donated their time to help me prepare for this. Also, I've worked harder than I've ever worked in my life. I can't wait to get back there!"

Ron smiled at me, then at the camera. "Well, Becki, we all wish you the very best, and we look forward to you bringing Idaho its first Miss America crown!"

Ron signed off with the station. After thanking the news people, the evening's coordinators, and my Treasure Valley board members, I returned home exhausted. But my exhaustion proved no match to my excitement.

As I tried to sleep, I went over the evening again in my mind. It came back to me in flashes. The photos, the music, the people. Most of all, I thought of the people. People of all ages, sizes, and backgrounds. Every one of them believed in me. I realized, again, how important my influence was.

"Lord, help me to remember that they not only judge *me* by my actions, but that people will judge *You* by my actions also. Help me to uphold Your name."

The words of encouragement came back to me. I remembered the hugs, the small token gifts. And as I thought of the Miss America competition, I knew I wouldn't be able to sleep for a while.

Quietly, I got out of bed and walked to the kitchen for a glass of water. I found my mother sitting at the dining-room table looking at my baby pictures. "Mom, what are you doing?" I asked as I filled my glass and walked to the table.

"Just remembering." She smiled at me and pointed to the pictures. "You almost didn't make it. I'd lost so many babies . . ." She paused and choked a little. "I always knew God had something special planned for you."

I smiled and sat beside her. I'd heard that story many times, but it always thrilled me. God had to have had a reason to let me live. I picked up a picture of me at six. "Look at this one," I handed the photo to my mother. "My hair is so blonde it looks white!"

Mom looked at the picture, smiled, and put it back with the others.

"We're very proud of you, Becki," she said quietly. "To see you onstage tonight, all those people who just wanted to meet you, well, I felt so proud you were my daughter."

I smiled gently at her, not wanting to say anything.

"But do you know what I'm most proud of? I'm most proud that you love the Lord. That means more to me than anything you have, or ever will accomplish."

For a few seconds, neither of us spoke. I looked at the pictures on the table. They represented a collage of my life. "Mom, are you scared? You know, of what will happen in Atlantic City?"

She turned and looked me directly in my eyes. "No, Becki, I'm not."

"But you've lived this whole experience with me," I said. "You've worked almost as hard as I have! Have you wondered what will happen if I don't win?" I looked earnestly at her.

"No, I'm leaving everything in God's hands," she replied. "All along I've prayed for His will to be done, and I believe, without a doubt, that it *will* be done. I believe God has put you in this position. I know you *can* be Miss America, but if things don't work out that way, I know God has a plan anyway."

I hugged her and sat quietly. For a few minutes, only the ticking of the clock broke the silence. Finally, yawning, I stood up and stretched. "I guess I'd better try to get some sleep." Covering my mouth to stop another yawn, I turned to leave the room, but stopped at the door. Facing my mother again, I felt a rush of love.

"Goodnight, Mom," I whispered. "I love you."

"I love you too, Becki."

Chapter 7

The Send-off

The night before flying to Atlantic City, I left my parents' home and stayed with Leanne, my traveling companion. The entire day before, my aunts and grandmother had helped me pack. I felt too excited to sleep. I worried about my clothes. Did I pack the right ones? Would I be appropriately dressed for everything? To keep calm I imagined the announcer calling my name as the new Miss America, but that only got me more excited.

Early the next morning, Leanne and I waited impatiently for the limousine that would take me to the airport. Five minutes, then ten. No limousine.

"Do you think we should call the company?" Leanne asked her husband Tom.

"I doubt anyone will be there this early in the morning," he said.

I looked at the clock. Five in the morning. We waited a few more minutes. Leanne checked her watch.

"You'd better drive us there," she told Tom. "We can't afford to wait any longer."

We squeezed my fifteen pieces of luggage and Leanne's few suitcases into the car and drove to the airport.

We arrived at the airport at five-thirty and piled all the luggage on a cart. Leanne checked it in and got our tickets while I smiled and greeted people. Close to fifty people swarmed around wearing pink T-shirts with my picture on them.

"I can't believe all these people showed up this early in the morning just to see me off," I murmured to my parents, who'd shown up to see me off too. "This is so nice!"

It seemed like everyone hugged me and kissed my cheeks. Their excitement made mine even more intense. People gave me letters, cards, and small gifts.

Leanne returned with our tickets. "We're flying first class," she informed me. "In Chicago we'll change planes."

I barely heard her. Everyone around me talked excitedly, and the pink T-shirts kept catching my attention. It felt strange to see my face on other people's shirts.

We all walked toward the gate area. Friends, aunts, uncles, grandparents—everyone was there to support and care. When we reached the gate, I gasped, surprised. Banners and signs hung on the walls. The biggest one caught my attention.

"Today Miss Idaho, Tomorrow Miss America!"

I hugged my family tightly. They all seemed so excited for me.

"We are now boarding first class for flight 610 to Chicago," an agent announced over the airport's sound system.

His smooth voice brought me quickly back to reality. Mom looked at me and smiled, tears in her eyes. Dad held out his arms for a hug.

"We'll be praying for you every day," he said as I wrapped my arms around him.

Mom put her arms around me too, and we stood for a few seconds just holding each other.

"We'll see you after the preliminaries, OK?" Mom smoothed my hair with one hand.

I hugged them both, afraid I'd start crying. "I've got to get on the plane . . ."

They kissed my cheeks, and I pulled away. Gathering my purse and carry-on bag, I slowly walked to the entrance of the jetway. As I got to the door, I turned and waved goodbye. The going-away group waved. My aunts and uncles blew kisses. My parents just stood and watched me. As I turned and walked briskly toward the plane, I wondered what they were thinking. Were they as scared as I felt?

Boarding the plane, I could feel my world shrinking. Now I had only Leanne, my traveling companion, to confide in. The pageant suddenly seemed very real and very close.

The plane took off at six-thirty. The other passengers in first class had seen the signs in the airport and wanted to talk. "What are you doing for your talent number?" one lady asked.

"I'm singing 'God Bless the U.S.A.'," I replied.

"Have you ever been in any pageants before you won Miss Idaho?" a man interjected.

"Except for winning my preliminary competition to Miss Idaho, no. This is my first one."

"Well, I'll be watching for you when the pageant airs," the woman said. "I hope you win!"

"I hope I do too!" I replied, laughing.

After we leveled off, the stewardess sat down across the aisle from me.

"What made you want to try for Miss America?" she asked.

"It's a long story," I replied, "but I guess I really wanted a challenge. And this has been a *huge* challenge!"

Another passenger pressed a call button, and the stewardess jumped up to answer it. I leaned back in my seat and opened one of the cards the people in the airport had given me. The cover of the card had huge gold script that spelled out "Best Wishes!" Inside, a stranger had penned a personal note. "Becki," it said, "we'll be praying for you.

You're going to do GREAT in Atlantic City!!"

I smiled and reached for another card. It had a similar message. I'd just started reading a third card when the stewardess returned to her seat across from me. "Have you seen this article?" she asked, handing a magazine to me. "One of the other passengers thought you might be interested in reading it."

"Thanks!" I smiled at her and accepted the magazine.

The stewardess walked to the back of the plane to begin serving breakfast. I sighed and opened the magazine. The article title seemed to jump off the page at me.

"Leanne! Have you seen this?" I nudged my traveling companion urgently.

Silently we looked at the article. A beautiful, smiling girl stared back at us under the article title, "Miss Missouri: the next Miss America?"

I read the article feverishly, eager to glean any information I could about this girl. A veterinary student, Debbye Turner was this journalist's choice for Miss America. I stared at her face again, and a strange feeling came over me. *I* was going to be the next Miss America. What was this girl's picture doing with this article?

Or *was* I going to be the next Miss America? I struggled with doubts. Perhaps I wouldn't win. I looked again at the cards in my lap and remembered how I'd felt called by God to pursue the Miss America crown.

"Oh, Lord," I breathed silently. "Help me to keep my strength, courage, and faith up. Help me to remember You're in charge here."

Feeling a little stronger, I handed the magazine back to the stewardess as she passed.

"How could someone give you something like that to read?" Leanne asked. "It's the last thing you, or any other contestant, wants to see when you're flying back to the competition!"

"No kidding," I agreed.

I picked up more of the cards and read them. They failed to calm me. I knew I was the best I'd ever been in every area. I couldn't be more ready, but I still felt unprepared. My usual trick of imagining my name being called as Miss America didn't work either. Finally, I tucked the letters and cards back in my flight bag, leaned the seat back, and closed my eyes. "It's all begun, Lord," I prayed silently. "As soon as the plane left the ground I felt uneasy, and now I'm scared. This whole thing is totally out of my control."

I paused and could almost hear God's answer. "Yes, but is it out of Mine?"

"But I've worked so hard. I believe You're in control, but I'm scared. I don't know what I'm flying into."

"There will be times when it's hard to see, but I know what's best for you."

I hummed what now had become my theme song. The stewardess nudged my elbow with a cart. "Would you like breakfast?" she asked cheerily.

Leanne and I both nodded.

She handed both of us trays with steaming scrambled eggs and hash browns.

"You want coffee, tea, any kind of juice?"

"I'll take orange juice," Leanne answered.

"Coffee for me," I added.

She handed us both our drinks and wheeled to the next row. I felt too nervous to eat, but I knew I had to keep my strength up. I picked up my fork and tasted the eggs.

"Not bad." I took another bite, then set the fork down. "I just wish I wasn't so nervous. I don't feel I can eat a bit."

Leanne smiled and took a forkful of her hash browns. "Just wait until you taste the food they feed you back in Atlantic City. The pageant really believes in wining and dining its girls!"

"Yeah, and probably testing our willpower to see

which of us will eat too much of it and look terrible in the swimsuit and evening gown competitions!" I joked. I'd been carefully fitted into my evening gown a week ago. Even one extra ounce would show.

I picked at my breakfast, the stewardess came by and picked up our trays, and I leaned my seat back again and tried to sleep. Images and thoughts clamored for my attention. I remembered pledging my life to God as a young child. With unswerving childish faith I believed He had great things for me to do. And all through my growing-up years, even during high school, I'd kept that faith. Now, as I listened to the hum of the plane's engines, I knew I still believed. No matter what happened in Atlantic City, God had plans for my life.

I heard the lady across the aisle unbuckle her seat belt, and I felt her brush past me. I smiled, remembering her earlier curiosity, and wondered how really famous people like actors and musicians ever got any privacy.

"Would you like anything to drink?"

I opened my eyes and smiled up at the stewardess. "No thanks, I'm fine."

"Nothing for me," Leanne added.

I closed my eyes again and remembered my family. With a sudden rush, I wished they could be here with me. They had seen every up and down. They had watched me work harder than I'd ever worked in my life. They believed in me, unconditionally. I fought back the tears as I recalled their goodbye in the airport. I'd felt as I boarded the plane that they were as reluctant to let me go as I was to leave. We'd all worked for this moment, yet when the time came, they wanted to protect me a little longer, and I wanted to stay in that protection. None of us really knew what Atlantic City would bring.

"God," I prayed silently. "Please give me strength and courage. You're the only one left for me to rely on. Please help the other girls see Jesus in me."

I opened my eyes and looked out the plane window. The morning sunshine lighted the white fluffy clouds beneath us, making them look like cotton candy. I imagined one cloud to be shaped like a horse. Another looked just like a person's face. Laughing a little at my active imagination, I felt my nervousness slowly give way to excitement.

"This is going to be the greatest adventure of your life," I promised myself.

I took out the going-away cards and letters I hadn't looked at yet, and read them the rest of the way into Chicago.

Chapter 8

Trump Castle

"We would like to thank you for flying with . . ." The flight attendant's voice sounded cheerful over the cabin's public address system as the plane slowly moved toward the gate. I looked excitedly out the window. Miss South Dakota, whom we'd joined in Chicago, looked just as excited as I felt.

"Please remain seated until the captain turns off the no smoking sign."

After what seemed an interminable length of time, we were let off the plane. Leanne got our luggage off the conveyer belt. I automatically grabbed two of my suitcases before she stopped me.

"No, Becki, you're not supposed to carry your own luggage. We'll get the driver to help us."

I looked up to see a uniformed chauffeur coming toward us. He and Leanne worked through the airport crowd with all the luggage while I followed, feeling rather silly. I'd always carried my own bags.

The chauffeur led us out of the airport to a taxi area where a long white limousine sat waiting. After piling the luggage in the back, Leanne snapped a picture of me standing with my hand on the car. I climbed into the back seat and admired the opulent luxury. "Well, well, well," I commented as Leanne sat down beside me and shut the door. "A phone and everything!"

"Didn't I tell you the Miss America Pageant people spoil their girls?" Leanne asked, grinning. "Enjoy it!"

I ran my hand over the crushed velvet seats and stretched my legs out. My feet barely reached the seat in front of me. I pushed one button and watched a window close us off from the driver. A miniature TV sat in front of us, and there was a stereo beneath the TV. I opened the small refrigerator at my feet and gasped.

"Hungry?" I asked Leanne, pointing to the fully stocked fridge. "How about a little caviar, or perhaps some champagne?"

Leanne laughed and pulled a notebook out of her bag.

"What's that?" I asked, pointing to the notebook.

"Your itinerary," she replied, not looking up from the page.

"Great, where do we go first?" I asked, realizing I didn't have any idea what I would be doing for the next few days.

"Hmm . . . we go to Trump Castle. That's where you'll be staying. And your Atlantic City hostess will greet us and take you to the convention center."

"I can't wait to get there," I sighed as I looked out the tinted windows of the limo. Everything seemed to move so slowly.

After touring a little of Atlantic City, the limousine stopped at Trump Castle. I got out of the car and almost grabbed my luggage before I remembered not to. Entering the building, I noticed a large billboard set up in the lobby: "Trump Castle welcomes these state contestants."

Four pictures hung underneath. I noticed my picture first, then quickly noted that Miss California, Miss Alabama, and Miss Missouri would be staying in the Castle too. I looked quickly at the picture of Miss Missouri, remembering the article I'd read on the plane. What would Debbye Turner be like?

An efficient-looking woman greeted us warmly. "Welcome to Atlantic City, Rebecca. I'm your hostess. Please follow me."

She led us through the lobby, into the elevator, and to our rooms. I marveled at the opulence as we walked through the Castle. Thick plush carpet covered the floors, and huge chandeliers glittered from the ceilings. I couldn't believe that some people lived their entire lives in such luxury!

"How close will we be staying to the other girls?" I asked as the elevator whisked us up to our floor.

"All fifty-one contestants are spread out over the city," Leanne replied. "Here in Trump Castle, each of you will be staying on different floors. Security measures, you know."

The elevator stopped at our floor, and we stepped out. Our hostess led us to our rooms. Behind us a bell-boy, his cart piled high, brought in our luggage. After opening our door and wheeling the luggage in, he left.

"I'll be up in half an hour to take you to the convention center," my hostess promised.

I walked quickly through both adjoining rooms, admiring the view of Atlantic City from the large windows.

"How do you want to set this up?" I called to Leanne.

"Let's turn the smaller room into one huge closet," Leanne instructed. "We'll sleep in the big room."

She took the suitcases quickly to the small room and began unpacking. I itched to help her.

"Can't I at least help you hang clothes?" I asked.

She laughed. "Sure, you're just not supposed to be carrying your own luggage in public."

We unpacked quickly. As I came to my registration suit, Leanne had me get changed and touch up my hair and makeup. I talked to her from the bathroom. "Don't you think they're overdoing the security measures just a little?"

"Better get used to it," she called back. "From now on

you won't even be able to go to the restroom by your-self."

"Great," I muttered sarcastically.

After retouching my makeup and hair, I changed into my freshly ironed interview suit. I said little on the way to the convention center. I was about to see the stage I'd dreamed about for so long. I'd be meeting my competitors. My hostess seemed to understand and sat quietly.

The limousines stopped at the convention center, and I got out of the car with a confidence I didn't feel. Squaring my shoulders, I walked briskly into the hall. I stopped just inside the door and stared at the cavernous auditorium.

It looked like a huge gym with folding chairs set up all over it. A gigantic stage dominated one end, and with a shiver I realized I'd be walking on it, performing on it. For the first time, the competition seemed real.

My hostess tugged at my arm. "Come on," she urged. "You'll be signing in backstage."

She led me behind the stage to a section that looked like it had once been a garage. People milled in every direction. Pageant contestants, escorts, officials, everyone seemed to be going everywhere at once. She directed me to a table where a smartly dressed woman sat.

"Name and state, please," the woman said briskly.

"Rebecca Eileen Trueblood, Miss Idaho," I replied, looking around.

"Hmm . . . oh yes, here we are." She handed me a badge and smiled. "Now if you'll just sign right here to say that you've arrived."

I took the badge and signed the paper.

"Now we need you to write a message on your state." She glanced up at a large map. "After that, visit each press table." She pointed to a large room behind her where photographers and reporters lined the walls.

"Thanks!" I fastened the badge carefully to my suit and walked over to the map. Pulling down Idaho, I stared at it for a second. "What should I say?" I wondered to myself. I thought of our centennial celebration coming up in a year and decided to write something about that. I looked at the state a minute, then wrote, "Happy Birthday Idaho! Celebrating 100 Years."

After putting Idaho back on the map, I turned and entered the press conference room. Tables lined the walls, and the contestants went from table to table answering questions. I smiled and said hello to a few other girls, wishing I had time to talk and get to know them. After figuring out which direction everyone was going around the press tables, I walked to the first table confidently.

"Give them something memorable," I inwardly reminded myself. "They won't quote boring things in the paper."

The questions started as soon as I reached the first table.

"What do you think should be done to combat the drug problems in America today?"

"How should our government address the homeless problem?"

"Do you think racial problems are worse or better than they were twenty years ago?"

Washington Post, New York Times, USA Today—all the major papers asked questions. The big fashion magazines like *Vanity Fair, Cosmopolitan*, and *Ebony* also interviewed each girl. Everyone seemed to hang on every word I uttered.

In the two hours it took to go to each press table, I answered more questions and defended myself on more issues than I ever had before. And through it all I kept reminding myself to give memorable answers and to smile. Photographers snapped pictures and reporters fired questions. Energy seemed palpable in the room.

After finishing my interview at the last table, I rejoined my hostess and a security escort.

"What's next?" I asked, excited.

"We're going back to the Castle to eat and get some sleep," the hostess replied briskly. "You've got a big day ahead of you tomorrow."

Reluctantly I left the activity of the pressroom and followed her and the escort back to the limousine. I felt so high I didn't think I'd ever be able to sleep that night. But I'd only been in the car about five minutes when I felt my energy being replaced by exhaustion.

"I'm so *tired*," I complained to Leanne as I came back into our rooms. "Just back at the convention center I felt I could keep going all night!"

Leanne laughed. "What did you expect after leaving Boise so early this morning and jumping two time zones?"

"Is it all going to be this exhausting?" I asked, collapsing on the bed as I spoke.

"Worse," Leanne promised.

I sat for a few minutes, then made myself get up and do my exercises. After an hour of working out, I studied my interview notes. Studying was the only real thing that comforted me and boosted my confidence. Finally, I prepared for bed quickly, mechanically, thinking only of sliding between cool sheets and going to sleep. I climbed into bed, said a quick sleepy prayer, and drifted off before Leanne had a chance to turn out the lights in the room.

She woke me early the next morning. After getting me out of bed and into the shower, she ordered breakfast and set out my rehearsal clothes. I stepped out of the steamy bathroom with a huge towel wrapped around me. I dressed quickly in my regulation jeans and red-and-white Miss Idaho T-shirt. I munched a

Childhood

Becki when she is seven years old

Heritage Singers

A happy time

Becki is in the center

Miss Treasure Valley

Becki won her first contest as
Miss Treasure Valley

Miss Idaho 1989

Getting ready for the pageant

Winning the Miss Idaho contest was a thrilling occasion for the whole family

Leaving for Atlantic City

The Miss America Pageant

Signing in, riding in the parade

Miss IDAHO

The swimsuit and evening
gown competitions;
with new friends

Singing was great;
losing was hard

Reigning as Miss Idaho

The Idaho National Guard enjoyed posing with Becki

Life as Miss Idaho had its fun moments

Baccalaureate speaker at a high-school graduation

Idaho's governor Cecil Andrus poses with Becki in his office

Passing on the crown

At the 1990 pageant Becki sang and crowned the new Miss Idaho

piece of toast as I stood in front of the mirror and did my makeup and hair.

"Are you going to the convention center with me today?" I called to Leanne in the next room.

"No, you'll be going with several other girls and your hostess."

I spritzed my hair with hairspray and put a final pat of powder on my nose.

"Your travel partners will be Miss California, Miss Alabama, and Miss Missouri," Leanne informed me.

"Miss Missouri? The one in the article on the plane?" I asked.

"The very one," she replied.

I finished my breakfast and preparation in silence. Bodyguards arrived to escort me to the car. I wondered about the other girls. What would they be like? What were their strengths and weaknesses?

I met them in the lobby of Trump Castle. They stood wearing jeans and shirts that matched mine exactly except that their shirts had their states on them. We gave each other friendly smiles and brief hellos before our hostess hurried us through the lobby to the car. People in the lobby stared, and some of them came up and asked for our autographs. Our hostess pushed us quickly to the car.

"Whew!" I breathed as the limousine pulled into the traffic. "I can't believe all this!"

"I know what you mean," Debbye replied.

"It's good to finally meet some of the other girls!" I smiled across the car at her. "I'm Becki Trueblood."

The other girls smiled and introduced themselves. Miss California and Miss Alabama started talking, and I turned to Debbye.

"I read an article about you on the plane. It was very nice."

"Thank you," she replied. She paused slightly. "I'm

sure whatever you read was spiced up a little by the press, though."

The car stopped outside the convention center. We were escorted inside, again through a throng of reporters. Onstage, groups of beautiful girls stood around talking, all wearing outfits identical to mine. A coordinator came out, clapping his hands for attention. I settled on the floor of the stage with the other girls.

"We have just a little over a week to perfect three dance numbers," the coordinator began. "I want each of you to realize how serious you must be. People all over the United States and the world will be watching you on the final night. One wrong step and everyone sees it."

He stopped and took a clipboard from his assistant.

"As you already know, you'll be divided into three groups: Mu, Sigma, and Alpha. You've each received notices of which group you'll be in. Therefore, I'd like the Alpha group on the right of the stage, Mu group on the left, and Sigma in center. Find your group, ladies!"

I got up and joined the Mu group. We looked at each other, wondering if we should sit again or stay standing. When everyone had found her group, the director gave more instructions.

"My assistants and I will be working with one group at a time. When your group is not working, please stay close by so we don't have to waste time searching for you when your turn comes." He referred to his clipboard again. "We'll start rehearsal today with the Sigma group."

The other Mu group members and I sat down on the stage and watched the Sigma people learn their steps. I sighed, realizing we'd be doing a lot of sitting around for the next week.

"I always thought we'd be busy all day," I remarked to Miss Louisiana. "I wish I'd brought my camera."

"Bring it tomorrow. I'm sure things will move at

about the same pace then!" She squinted at my T-shirt. "Ah, Miss Idaho! I'm Stacy King."

"Becki Trueblood," I replied warmly. I liked her Southern accent. "What was your state pageant like?" I asked.

"It was wonderful! It was the most fun night of my life."

I smiled, remembering how much I'd enjoyed my own pageant, and wondered if the Miss America final night would be as much fun.

Practice continued until noon, when we broke for lunch. I talked to as many other girls as I could. Everyone seemed so confident and poised. And like at the Miss Idaho competition, I felt surprised at how nice everyone seemed. I asked lots of questions, and everyone seemed eager to talk.

The afternoon consisted of more practicing and sitting around. By the end of the day I'd learned the steps to one dance number and made several new friends.

The other girls and I spoke little in the car on the way back to Trump Castle. I thought of everything that had happened during the day, all the people I'd met. It didn't feel like a competition. As I looked at my traveling companions and remembered Stacy and the other girls I'd made friends with, I determined to be as real and genuine with them as I could.

Chapter 9

Glitz, Glamour, and Royal Treatment

The official registration. All the winners from the fifty states and the District of Columbia dressed in their best finery and introduced themselves to the press and the pageant officials. Even though the program wasn't open to the general public, I could feel the excitement and confidence radiating from all the other girls, and knew I projected the same energy.

From his place behind a microphone, an announcer greeted the audience. "Good evening, ladies and gentlemen of the press. Tonight is the official registration. Tonight the Miss America Pageant 1989 is declared officially open!"

People applauded, flashbulbs went off, and one by one the girls started introducing themselves.

"I'm Miss Alabama!"

"I'm Miss Alaska!"

I watched each girl introduce herself and identify her state. Each one seemed so perfect. As I listened to each introduction, watched every smile, I knew that any one of these girls possessed the attributes of a great Miss America.

I walked confidently to the microphone and smiled brilliantly.

"I'm Miss Idaho, Rebecca Eileen Trueblood!"

More introductions, more smiles, more applause. The whirl of pretty girls and beautiful gowns grew dizzying. I wondered, as I watched each one, did they have any insecurities? Were they ever as burned out about competing as I felt sometimes? Somehow I knew, as I looked at their perfect, smiling façades, that I wouldn't get to know the true people behind the masks.

As the evening ended, the press people asked questions of the girls and took pictures. Miss Oklahoma and I posed together as the two oldest contestants in the pageant. Everywhere I went, people asked more questions.

Inside I felt great. Back in Idaho, my board members told me that the press follows the girls they think will win. I knew I didn't get more attention than the other girls, but I also knew I wasn't receiving any less. I went back to Trump Castle feeling very high that night.

The royal treatment continued. Every time the other girls and I stepped out of the building the next day, the press descended on us. I answered their questions carefully, always trying to say something memorable and worthwhile. I didn't want to start getting bad press!

The night after the official registration, Merv Griffin and Eva Gabor hosted a party for all the contestants. Knowing this would rival royal elegance, I dressed and prepared carefully. "What do you think?" I asked Leanne, turning in front of her several times.

"It's perfect," she decreed.

I eyed myself in the full-length mirror, critically checking for flaws. My fitted maroon dress looked very simple and plain in the front. The back dropped and had sequins all over it. Sighing, I plucked at the skirt. I'd been worried all along about having the right clothes.

The limousine picked us up at Trump Castle and took us to Merv Griffin's hotel. The chauffeur opened the door for me, and I gasped as I stepped out on a plush red carpet. Officers from a nearby naval base lined the carpet, their swords making a canopy for us to walk under.

An escort took my arm. "We'll be following that couple right there," he whispered.

I watched, amazed, as each girl got escorted in one by one. When my turn came, I walked carefully down the carpet to the entrance. The swords glinted in the lights from the hotel.

Once inside the door, cheerleaders did cheers. My escort led me to the stage, where all the girls waited to meet Eva. Merv would be announcing our names, but he couldn't see any of us because he would be judging the pageant. I noticed he wore a blindfold. As we stood there, I studied the banquet hall.

Live island music underscored the tropical room. I looked at the lush palm trees, vibrant flowers, and rich vegetation. It seemed warmer and steamier in here than any other building in Atlantic City. I could almost hear the lapping of waves.

People filled the room. Some of the guests were connected with the pageant. Others were wealthy people visiting Atlantic City for the summer. I had never seen so many glamorously dressed people before in my life!

The introductions began. Merv Griffin greeted his guests, then began introducing each contestant individually from behind his blindfold. Eva Gabor gave each one a kiss and a flower. I waited my turn patiently, drinking in the beauty and opulence of the room.

The girl before me ran through her introduction quickly. I walked past Merv, smiling, feeling the excitement and fun of the evening.

"This is Rebecca Eileen Trueblood, Miss Idaho!" Merv announced.

I smiled and greeted Eva. She handed me a rose and gave me a kiss on the cheek.

On the other side of the stage, my escort greeted me again and led me to my place at one of the tables. The introductions continued until each girl had been presented and greeted. Then, with great ceremony, the feast began.

Sumptuous food appeared, everything perfectly prepared for taste, smell, and sight. The waiters catered to every need, wish, and whim. A bread waiter brought only breads, a water waiter replenished everyone's glasses, a drinks waiter took orders, food waiters whisked away plates almost before I'd finished eating off them. I ate sparingly, never forgetting I had to fit into my evening gown.

As I finished eating, I looked around the elegant room, trying to memorize it. I wanted to remember everything so that I could share it with my family when I saw them again.

The rest of the week blurred by in a whirl of sumptuous banquets, press attention, and frenzied activity. The reality of competition seemed far off. I tried to get to know some of the other girls.

"What made you try for Miss America?" I asked Debbye one morning as we rode together to the convention center.

"Well, you know I've tried to win a state title for seven years now," she replied. "I guess I just don't give up easily!"

I laughed at her candid reply.

"I also wanted to do it for the scholarships," she continued. "Veterinary school is very expensive. But most of all I wanted to be Miss America because I want to show that a girl who had nothing can become something. I want to use it as a chance to share my faith in God."

I felt surprised at her answer. When I first won Miss Idaho, I thought I'd be one of the few Christian girls involved in the pageant. Debbye not only was Christian, but she had a similar message she wanted to share. And I also wanted to tell kids that they could become something if they tried hard enough.

As I got to know more of the girls, I found that many of them were Christians. Many of them, like myself, had felt called to enter the pageant. Many of them had people praying for them. Any one of these Christian girls would use the office of Miss America to witness for God.

The fun, parties, and banquets slowed down as we got closer to the actual competition. I noticed the girls beginning to close off more. Everyone, including myself, began feeling the pressure of competition. No one wanted to show any insecurities, and I found the perfect façades daunting. I knew I had faults, but I couldn't seem to see any in anyone else. Logically, I knew each girl had her problem area. My insecurities made it hard to remember that, though. It became increasingly difficult to be natural and real with everyone.

"Lord," I prayed often. "Help me keep my focus on You. It's so exciting here, the competition has to be the focus of all my thoughts. Please help me not to forget You."

It felt strange to know that the other Christian girls in the pageant were probably praying the same prayer.

Chapter **10**

The Interview

I woke early the day of my interview. The former carefree feeling of the competition had vanished, and I suddenly felt shot into reality. In a week, a new Miss America would be crowned, and I knew that if it was to be me I'd have to concentrate.

I ate breakfast in silence, with my interview notebook in hand, going over all the things I'd studied during the summer. After showering, I dressed carefully in my interview outfit.

Of all my outfits, I'd chosen this one most carefully. I knew a lot of girls would be dressing extravagantly for their interviews, but I deliberately chose very simple clothes. I wanted the judges to see my face, not what I had on.

I stood in front of the mirror as I tucked my green turtle-necked blouse into my black skirt and circled my waist with a wide belt. I added very few accessories.

My escorts arrived at the door just as I finished styling my hair. I greeted them and walked to the car quickly. I sat silently all the way to the convention center.

We arrived at the center, and my escorts took me to a huge room where all the contestants waited their turn. As it came closer to my interview time, I found myself led out of the convention center to a casino next door. We waited in this room for a little longer. Eventually I was pointed down a huge empty hallway to a final waiting room just outside the interview room. I listened to my high heels tap on the bare floors as I walked down the hall. My mind raced to remember everything I'd learned.

I walked into the final waiting room. The girl who had her interview before me sat waiting, and the girl who was to go after me walked in the door just after I did. I sat and waited nervously.

"Help me to remember everything I learned this summer," I prayed.

I took deep breaths and tried to relax. A contestant came out of the interview room, a big smile on her face. The girl before me was escorted in to see the judges.

"How'd it go?" I asked the girl who'd just finished her interview.

"Great! I loved it!" she gushed.

"Oh, great," I thought to myself. "If she did that well, I'll have to work even harder!" I determined to make the judges laugh right off the bat.

My turn came at last. The contestant in front of me left the interview room, and an escort led me in. A bright spotlight shone from the top of the room. Video cameras sat underneath. Timers sat on one side of the room, pageant officials on the other. The judges sat right underneath me.

I blinked at the bright lights. Everything seemed kind of blurry. My escort introduced me to the judges.

"I'd like you to meet Rebecca Eileen Trueblood, Miss Idaho!"

The judges didn't respond. I drew a deep breath and flashed my most brilliant smile. I knew I could make them laugh.

"I'm so glad this part is finally here. I've been working on this so long, and I'm glad to finally meet all of you!"

No one laughed. The judges just looked at me. I walked quickly to the interview chair and started to sit down. Their first questions began before I had even finished sitting down.

"Rebecca, we believe liberalism in the United States is declining. If you agree with us, give three reasons supporting that. If you disagree, give us three reasons why."

I sat down quickly and answered the question. As soon as I finished, another judge fired another question at me. I gave the best answer I could, trying to think of ways to tell them a little about myself. I knew this would be the only time I'd meet personally with the judges. Each question I answered, I tried to interject a little about my travels.

The judges shot questions at me so fast that my seven minutes seemed more like seven seconds. When my time ended, I thanked the judges and turned to walk out of the room. I'd reached the door when I felt one of my shoes stick to the floor. I glanced down and tried to pull it off the video camera tape. It didn't budge. Nonchalantly, I stepped out of my shoe and kept walking.

I walked into the waiting room with a straight face. We'd been taught all along that if we ever lost a shoe to keep walking. Someone nudged my elbow. I looked into the laughing face of the security guard.

"I thought you might want this." He handed me my shoe.

"Thanks." I took the shoe from him, laughing.

The girls in the waiting room looked at me like they didn't know whether to laugh or not.

At rehearsal that afternoon, I tried to talk to some of the girls who'd done their interviews in the morning. Since my interview I'd gone over every question and every answer in my mind several times. I knew I hadn't done too badly, but I knew I hadn't blown them away either.

"How did your interview go?" I asked one girl.

"I loved it," she replied enthusiastically. "It was so much fun!"

I looked at her smiling face, so confident. But as I looked in her eyes, I could tell that she felt as insecure as I did about her interview. No one would admit it, though, and after a while I started to get worried. What if their interviews *had* gone that well?

I noticed Jennifer Wahl, Miss Washington, listening to the other girls rave about their interviews. I'd been at her pageant and felt I knew her pretty well. She stood away from the group, looking upset. I walked over to her.

"Jennifer, how was your interview?" I asked, putting my hand on her arm.

"OK, but the other girls are saying theirs were so wonderful. I know mine wasn't that wonderful." She turned to me, her eyes scared. "All I want is to be in top ten, Becki. All I want is to be in top ten."

I squeezed her arm. "Jennifer, those girls are probably just as nervous as we are. You'll make top ten," I promised.

"So will you," she offered back.

I looked at the girls talking excitedly about their interviews and knew, suddenly, that they felt just the same as Jennifer and I did. We were all on equal footing—no one had any guarantees. But even though I knew that, their false confidence began to work on me, and I could feel my own confidence dip a little.

My traveling companions and I rode back to Trump Castle that night together. I sat quietly, looking out the window. I glanced at Debbye and noticed she leaned against the back of the seat looking exhausted.

"Are you as tired as I feel?" I asked, smiling.

"Yeah, that was a lot of work today," she replied.

"I'm sure you did a great job," I told her.

She smiled. "Thanks."

We sat quietly for a few minutes. I listened to Miss Alabama and Miss California talk. I kept thinking of how all the other girls sounded so confident after their interviews.

"Do you think they did as well as they said they did?" I asked.

"What do you think?" Debbye asked quietly, grinning.

"I know, I know, it's just hard to take the mind games," I replied, stretching my arms above my head.

Debbye leaned across the car and put her hand on my arm. "Becki, don't worry about the other girls. You possess all the characteristics of a great Miss America. You'll do great!"

"Thanks, Deb, so will you."

I smiled at her, wondering how she could offer encouragement when some of the other girls felt afraid to. My respect for Debbye rose.

We arrived at Trump Tower, and I went straight to my room. As I prepared for bed, I thought through the events of the day. I knew that if I let them, the mind games of other people would erode my confidence. For survival in the pageant, I had to shut out everything except winning.

My mind struggled with that, though. All along I'd wanted to get away from the idea of acting like a competitor. I wanted to stay the same person through the whole pageant. It was getting harder and harder to do that, because I knew that in order to win, I needed to be competitive. For we all knew that in a week a new Miss America would be crowned, and only one of us would take home the crown.

Chapter 11

The Evening Gown and Swimsuit Competitions

Although neither the evening gown nor the swimsuit competitions proved heavily important for points, I felt even more the strain of competition. The other girls seemed to feel it too—most withdrew further behind their smiles. Winning the crown became everyone's sole focus. The tension began to show in small ways.

"Can we get this going?" one contestant complained for the third time in an hour.

I gritted my teeth and willed her to be quiet. We'd been rehearsing all afternoon, and her impatience really irritated me.

"We don't have time to waste," she added for emphasis.

I wondered how she could be so uptight about practicing the opening number. It wasn't the most important thing we were doing back here.

"Remember, Becki, she's under a lot of pressure," I reminded myself silently. "Just like you, she's worked hard for this." I reminded myself of that every time she complained. It usually kept me from getting too annoyed with her.

The night of the evening gown competition arrived.

81

Backstage in the dressing room, I expected noise and excited laughter. Instead, no one spoke. Each girl had her own mirror. We sat in our Mu, Sigma, and Alpha lines. Stacy sat on one side of me, Miss Michigan on the other. Although we were physically close to each other, each sat in our own little world. I, too, closed off and focused on the competition.

"Keep it pretty natural," I instructed the makeup artist, who busily brushed eye shadow on my lids.

"You'll look gorgeous," she replied as she began working on my cheeks.

She finished my face and had me look in the mirror for approval.

"It's great," I lied.

"Good luck tonight!" She moved on to another girl.

I looked at my reflection and grabbed a tissue. I knew I didn't have time to completely redo what she'd done, but I tried to touch it up as best I could. After a few attempts at changing the makeup, I decided I'd done the best I could.

"I'll do it myself tomorrow night," I whispered silently.

The evening's competition began with all the final night numbers. The only thing different was that we only had the evening gown competition instead of all areas. As I listened to the announcer and watched the lights, I wondered what it would feel like on the final night. I couldn't wait.

On stage, I did my trained walk and much-practiced turns. As I came by the judges, I smiled brilliantly at them. Each girl got to walk the runway. I found that that was my favorite part. The judges sat close to the stage, so once I got past them I didn't have to feel so tense, and I looked for my family in the audience. They sat together in a group, cheering and blowing kisses at me. I smiled broadly at them.

The competition went on. I couldn't wait to see my family. It seemed like a lifetime since I'd said goodbye to them in Boise. As soon as we performed the last number and the curtain fell, the other girls and I were escorted into a big room where all our family and friends waited. I went in and discovered everyone separated by state. Each group called to their girl. The noise level was deafening. I looked eagerly around the room for my supporters.

"Becki!" I turned swiftly and saw my family and friends waiting for me in a group. I ran to them and hugged my parents enthusiastically.

"How was your interview?" they asked.

"How did I look tonight?" I asked at the same time. We laughed.

"My interview went OK," I told them. "It's so good to see you guys!"

My grandmother came up and gave me a kiss. "You looked beautiful up there tonight, Becki."

"Are you sure?" I asked the whole family. "Tell me what I can do better tomorrow."

"You looked great," they assured me. I think they knew that's what I really needed to hear.

"How was your flight? What have you been doing since you all got here?" I knew I was asking too many questions, but it just felt so good to see them again.

We chatted for a few minutes about what they'd been doing all week. I told them about all the friends I'd made, the practicing, and the banquets. Almost too soon, a pageant official tapped my shoulder.

"It's time to leave." She stood and waited to escort me back to the car.

I didn't want to leave. I looked at my parents and felt I would burst with all I wanted to tell them.

"We'll see you tomorrow after swimsuit," they promised.

I reluctantly said goodbye and followed the sponsor out of the room. I gathered my things from the dressing room and was escorted to the waiting car. Outside, the press waited to talk to the girls. A few journalists asked me questions, but I noticed some of the other girls getting more attention. I tried not to let it bother me, but I kept remembering what my board members had told me: "The girls who get lots of press attention are the probable winners."

That night I prayed long and hard. Seeing the hope and pride my family had for me reminded me that they were just as emotionally tied up in the pageant as I was. They lived every competition I did. They scanned the papers for my quotes every day.

"Oh, God, help me not to disappoint them," I prayed. "We've come so far. They've prayed for this as much, or more, as I have."

I looked around the room at the gifts and flowers that had been arriving every day since the beginning of the pageant. My family had always believed I could do anything I wanted. Now they, my friends, and the people of Idaho all believed I would be the next Miss America. Their hopes rested on that belief as much as mine did. I vowed not to let anything deter me from doing my very best. I knew I'd done well so far. Now, at the halfway point, I determined to do even better.

The next day brought the swimsuit competition. We rehearsed all day, as usual, then did the full final night program again. I looked at the full auditorium and felt glad I'd done extra exercise all summer and avoided fattening food. I knew I'd never feel uncomfortable on a public beach again after this scrutiny. I did my walk and turns with practiced ease. And I smiled, knowing that after tonight, the worst was over. I looked forward to the talent competition.

After the final number, we were again able to see our

families. I grilled them on my appearance and performance.

"Are you sure I looked OK?" I asked anxiously. "What can I do better tomorrow night?"

"You looked wonderful," they continually reassured me.

"I am *so* excited about talent tomorrow night," I told my parents. "I can't wait to sing on that stage!"

"We'll take lots of pictures," Dad promised.

"Is there anything we can get you?" Mom asked. "Anything you need?"

"No, Mom, thanks, though. The pageant people get me everything. Don't worry about it."

"It's a mother's job to worry," Mom replied jokingly. "It makes me feel needed."

I hugged her tightly. "Oh, Mom, I need you and Dad *so much*. Every time I get tired or discouraged, it helps to know you're praying for me."

"We're not going to stop now," Dad promised.

For a few seconds no one spoke. I looked at my parents, my grandmother, my brother, my friends, and could feel tears forming. I needed these people so badly. I finally broke the silence. "Well, tomorrow's the final preliminary. After that . . ."

Mom squeezed my hand. "You're going to blow them away," she promised.

I laughed. "Well, maybe not blow them away, but at least I have more experience singing on stage than walking around in a swimsuit or evening gown looking beautiful!"

The sponsor came up and told me it was time to go. I looked at my family, tears in my eyes.

"Pray for me," I whispered.

"We never stopped," Mom replied tenderly. "Now go get some sleep so you can be gorgeous tomorrow."

I smiled and allowed myself to be escorted to the car.

As we drove back to Trump Castle, I looked at the bright lights of Atlantic City. The whole city seemed an advertisement for the Miss America contest. Lighted signs announced it, banners hung on buildings, everyone seemed caught up in the hype. I could feel my own excitement quickening at the thought of the final night.

I hummed a few bars of my talent number. I couldn't wait to sing it the next day.

Chapter **12**

The Talent Competition

After rehearsing all morning, each of us had ten minutes with the stage and sound system to go over our talent numbers. I sat in the audience and listened to the other girls run through their talents as I waited for my turn. Each one seemed better than the last. With a sense of growing dismay, I realized everyone was very, *very* good at what we did. I tried to block everything out and focus on my own number.

My rehearsal time finally arrived. I stood in the middle of the huge stage, microphone in hand, and waited for my music to start. The empty auditorium had folding chairs as far as I could see. I felt a thrill as I imagined how it would look full of people.

My tape started, and I came in at the wrong place.

"Could you cue it up again?" I asked into the microphone.

The tape began again, but my voice didn't open up, and I couldn't hit my high notes. I looked at my watch. Four minutes left.

"Can we try it one more time?" I asked nervously.

The tape started in the right place at the right time, and I sang through it fairly well. When my time was up, I reluctantly handed the microphone to the next girl and walked off the stage. I really felt I needed a few more times through to feel comfortable with the sound system and the stage.

I listened to more of the talent rehearsals for the rest of the afternoon. With each polished performance I could feel my confidence slipping a little.

"They're all so *good*," I thought.

I prayed for confidence. And instead of focusing on the other rehearsals, I reminded myself of all the years of experience I'd had performing with Heritage. I drew on that valuable experience now.

I thought of the song I'd chosen. It stretched me more vocally and dramatically than I'd ever stretched myself before. I'd practiced and perfected it all summer until I knew it was as good as it would ever be. It was ready. I was ready. My confidence returned, and I couldn't wait to sing that night.

The talent competition. Again we ran through everything like the final night. I knew I'd remember every number, every step, for the rest of my life. I looked at my family sitting in the audience. Their faces mirrored my eager anticipation. I waited backstage for my number. On stage I could hear the enthusiastic audience cheering for each number. When my name was finally announced, I whispered a quick prayer and stepped onto the stage.

I stood in the spotlight, holding a microphone, and waited for my tape to start. Miraculously it started in the right place and at the right level. I heard my cue and started singing. With each note, each word, my voice got stronger. I threw myself into the song.

". . . God Bless the U.S.A. . . ."

I came to the dramatic ending of the song and felt the audience's applause wash over me. I walked backstage, feeling a foot above ground. I knew I'd done my best.

"Thank You, Lord," I whispered. "Thank You."

I felt a release of tension, knowing that my preliminaries were through. The judges would make their decision on the top ten, and no matter what, I knew I'd done my best.

My family rushed to me afterwards. They knew how much the talent competition meant. "Becki, you sang so well!"

"I couldn't believe you weren't nervous up there. All those people, I would have died."

Everyone talked at once, and I drank in the excited babble. I glanced around the room and noticed that all the other girls and their families looked just as excited as we did. By now I was used to the routine, so I pulled myself away from them before the escort told me it was time to leave.

I kissed them all goodbye and let myself be escorted out of the convention center. Outside, photographers and reporters swarmed to a few of the girls. I could see Debbye was surrounded. I wasn't asked many questions. I grew worried. I tried to push the fear out of my mind, but it nagged at me.

In bed that night, I consoled myself that at least I wasn't getting any negative press. Some of the other girls were seeing terrible things about themselves in the paper. I had nothing to be ashamed of, but why didn't I get *more* attention?

The next day after practice, I sat and listened to the rest of the girls go over their talent numbers. All week I'd had Leanne get the papers for me, and I'd eagerly looked for any quotes or pictures of myself. At the beginning of the week, I'd been in the papers a lot. But I noticed the press's interest had shifted lately to other girls.

I flipped through a paper I'd brought in with me. Debbye's smile caught my attention. She'd been in the paper every day. A few other girls showed up repeatedly also. I noticed a few references to me and Miss Oklahoma for being the two oldest contestants. That was all that was said about me in the paper. A cold feeling came over me.

"I'm not going to win, am I, Lord?" I whispered.

I fought the feeling immediately. I'd been called to this. Lots of people were praying for me. The press wasn't always right. Nothing had been decided yet. But the feeling refused to go away. I knew, with cold certainty, that I wouldn't be bringing the crown back to Idaho. What would I do if I didn't win? I had barely considered the possibility.

"Help me to at least make top ten," I prayed. "I have to make top ten." I consoled myself that if I didn't win I was at least doing well enough for top ten. I'd get a chance to perform on national TV. Idaho would know they'd sent a winner back to Atlantic City to represent them.

"Lord, I've prayed all along that Your will be done. Please, Lord, I've felt this pageant has been Your will. I don't want to believe my negative feelings. I want to believe You're in control."

I went over every question I'd had in my interview, every move in the evening gown and swimsuit competitions, every note of my talent number. I knew I'd done my very best in all areas. I had to trust God; everything was now out of my hands.

Glancing down at Debbye's picture again, I remembered how she never seemed afraid to encourage me. I could be honest with her, and she was always honest back.

We talked a lot about our faith in God. Looking at her picture, I hoped we'd stay in touch after the pageant. I wondered what would happen if one of us made Miss America and the other didn't. For the entire pageant, all fifty-one girls were on the same level. After the pageant, the balance of power would change. Some of the girls, the ones who placed, would be above the others. If I became Miss America, would it change how I felt about Debbye? If she won, would she feel different?

Somehow I knew both of us were real enough that we'd be the same people after the pageant as now.

On stage, another girl began rehearsing her talent number. I looked at my watch. After tonight the judges would make their decisions. The top ten girls would be chosen. I prayed I'd be one of them.

Chapter **13**

The Miss America Parade

Friday night. The preliminary competitions were over. The judges had decided the top ten. None of us knew who had made the list, but the tension of competition had let up. Tonight was the last night of hype before the final pageant. I prepared for it with excitement.

"Is it cold out there?" I asked Leanne as I bobby-pinned my hat to my hair.

"Yeah, a little, and very windy," she replied. "You'd better put a few extra pins on your hat—you don't want it blowing out to sea!"

I anchored my hat firmly to my head, then surveyed myself in the full-length mirror. I loved this dress. I wore a forties-style black sequined suit and hat—one of my favorite outfits. I turned one last time and checked for runs in my nylons. Leanne gave her approval of my ensemble.

The convention center buzzed with the excitement of fifty-one animated contestants. I looked at the other girls and marveled at all the beautiful dresses. Pageant officials ran around trying to organize everyone. I posed for pictures with Debbye and a few of the other girls.

Outside the convention center, we could hear crowds gathering for the parade. A TV set sat in the corner of the room so we could watch the parade while waiting our turn to be part of it.

With much fanfare, the parade began. Miss Wyoming started the procession as the last state in the alphabet. We watched on TV as the crowds cheered each girl. The wind whipped at the crowd, but no one seemed to mind.

"I hope I get a red car," a girl across the room said.

"And a good-looking driver," someone else added.

We all laughed at the last comment. Ever since arriving in Atlantic City, we'd been carefully kept away from all men.

I looked at the TV and watched each girl wave from the back of her own antique convertible. Spotlights mounted on the front of every car highlighted each contestant. I remembered how much fun my going-away parade had been in Caldwell, and couldn't wait to get out into this one.

"Oh my goodness, it looks like Miss Oklahoma just got hit by something!" the girl sitting closest to the TV exclaimed.

All conversation in the room ceased, and we concentrated on the TV action.

"Is she OK?" someone finally whispered.

"What do you think hit her?" another girl asked.

We watched as escorts led Miss Oklahoma's car quickly out of the parade. A pageant official came into the room where we all sat, and we grilled her with questions.

"What happened?"

"Is she going to be all right?"

"There isn't some crazy out there taking pot shots at the girls, is there?"

She held up her hands to stop the questions.

"Miss Oklahoma was hit in the head with a bottle. We don't know who threw it. Security people are combing the area looking for anyone who might know what happened. You have nothing to worry about."

"But what about *her*? Is she OK?" the girl next to me pressed.

The pageant official hesitated a minute. "We've taken Miss Oklahoma to the emergency unit at the nearest hospital. She should be fine."

We looked at each other, stunned into silence.

"Now," she continued, "I need states K through M to follow me."

The designated girls followed her to their cars. The rest of us stared at each other for a few minutes. Someone finally asked the question we'd all been thinking. "I wonder if she'll be able to perform tomorrow night."

No one responded. I sat and wondered how it would feel to have come so far and be knocked out of the competition because of a flying bottle. All that work to have to watch the final night on TV from a hospital room! I prayed she'd be OK and able to make the pageant.

Working backward, the alphabet of states finally reached Idaho, and I joined the parade. I sat perched on the back seat of my open car, a spotlight shining fully in my face. I noticed the crowd had dispersed itself by state with each group of supporters wearing T-shirts of their girls. One could tell when a girl reached her group of supporters by the loud cheering that would erupt.

I held my hat on my head with one hand and waved to everyone with the other. The spectators waved and cheered back. Even though each group rooted its own girl, they all cheered the other fifty contestants for having come so far and accomplished so much.

The parade rolled slowly through the crowd. I waved and smiled, and after a while my arm started to get a little sore from being held up so long. I smiled at everyone, but searched carefully for my Idaho supporters. I knew they'd be wearing the pink T-shirts I'd seen in the airport when I flew out.

We rounded a corner, and loud cheering and applauding erupted on my right. The Idaho group, all wearing the expected pink T-shirts, screamed and jumped up and down as my car approached. I waved and blew kisses at them.

"We love you, Becki," someone called.

"You're doing great! You're a winner!"

"We'll be cheering you tomorrow night!"

I wanted to stay and talk to them, but the parade continued on. My supporters kept cheering until I rode out of sight.

The rest of the parade passed in a blur of excitement and encouragement. People I didn't know, people from many other states, yelled out words of encouragement as we passed. Cameras flashed, reporters called out questions. I could see the end of the parade coming, and I didn't want it to end. It felt so exciting to be in Atlantic City!

Chapter **14**

The Day Arrives

On the day of the final pageant, all the other girls and I were escorted to the convention center at seven o'clock in the morning and locked in. No one was let in or out. We knew the top ten list had been released and that everyone except the fifty-one contestants knew who had made it.

We ran through one last rehearsal of the group numbers and blocked our steps for TV. Through everything, a sense of unreality pervaded me. I couldn't believe that the day I'd worked for and imagined for so long had finally arrived. A table had been set up with food behind the stage, but no one touched it. I figured everyone else was as paranoid about weight as I was.

The rehearsal directors had each contestant walk the runway individually. We each learned where to stop and wave, where to smile for the TV cameras. No matter who won, we were all prepared to take the victory walk.

After spending the night before in intensive care, Miss Oklahoma joined us for practice. She looked pale and tired, and her escort made her lie down in the sleeping area that had been set up for the girls upstairs.

"Can you believe she got out of the hospital in time for this?" I remarked to Stacy, remembering how injured she'd been the night before.

"I'd hate to be in her place," Stacy commented. "I'm

97

tired from all the things we've done for the last two weeks. It would be ten times worse to be injured too."

Practice continued until four o'clock. A few of the girls went upstairs to the sleeping room to rest, and others stretched out on the stage and slept there. I felt too excited to sleep, so I watched the NBC network people setting up equipment for the pageant. I turned and watched Stacy come toward me. She sat down with a sigh and silently watched the TV crews work for a few seconds.

Finally she spoke. "Have you seen the huge bowl of popcorn they have on the table backstage?" she asked. "It looks *so good.*"

I, too, had been wistfully eyeing the popcorn. "Yeah, the first thing I'm going to do after the pageant is eat!"

Stacy laughed, nodding her head. We watched the set-up crew again, not speaking.

"What are you going to do when you get home?" she asked quietly.

I sighed. I didn't want to hear that question. I didn't want it to end. "I don't know," I replied. "Catch up on sleep, get in contact with all the friends I ignored while I prepared for this thing."

"It feels so strange to think I'll be on the plane going home tomorrow," she said, resting her chin on her hand.

I didn't want to think I'd be on a plane going home. I wanted to believe I'd be starting my reign as Miss America. I looked at Stacy and knew she felt the same way.

"How do you go back to a normal life after all this?" I asked. "All this excitement . . ."

We sat silently for a few minutes, each of us lost in our own thoughts. I tried to imagine flying home to Boise, settling back into the old routine. Out of all fifty-one girls at the pageant, only one of us wouldn't have to do that. She would keep living the dream world while the rest of us went back to reality.

Stacy shifted slightly. "I think I'll go and try to sleep. What time are you going to start getting ready?" She stood up and looked down at me while she spoke.

"Probably about seven." I glanced at my watch. I had several hours to kill before then.

"I guess I'll see you in the dressing room," Stacy said as she turned to go.

"Yeah, see ya later."

I sat for a few more minutes and watched the TV crews finalize their preparation. Finally I stood and stretched. I picked my way carefully around several sleeping girls, grabbed my interview notebook, and found a quiet corner to sit in. Opening the notebook, I remembered all the hours I'd spent compiling and studying it. "It had better pay off now," I thought as I began reviewing.

I tried to guess what the judges would ask the top ten girls on stage that night. It made me nervous to think that, should I make top ten, I'd be expected to answer an impromptu question on live national TV. I carefully studied and reviewed everything I'd learned.

At seven o'clock I began to get ready for the pageant. As I looked in the mirror, I couldn't believe the night had finally arrived. I had worked for this night for so long. We'd practiced every step of it for two weeks. I thought of all the friends who'd be watching from all over the world. It felt strange to think that any household in America could turn on the TV and watch the pageant if they wanted to.

Around me, the other girls quietly did their make-up and hair. No one spoke. I mentally went over everything I'd studied in my interview notebook, and carefully thought through every note of my song.

I did my own make-up and hair, pulling on everything I'd learned about looking good on TV. A pageant official came into the dressing room.

"Half an hour, girls!"

I could feel nervousness and excitement rushing through me. Outside the dressing room we could hear music playing, the low rumble of the growing audience. My eyes glittered with excitement as I put my dress on.

"Oh God, this is it," I half thought, half prayed.

I could feel the energy of the other girls as we lined up in our lines. The audience's excitement felt like a live, palpable thing. My heart raced, and I realized my hands shook. "This is it!" I thought.

The music grew louder, more energetic. Pageant officials and escorts led my group to our designated starting point. A clock backstage registered three minutes to ten o'clock. I squeezed my hands together tightly and fought back tears.

"Be with me, Lord," I whispered.

Chapter 15

The Miss America Pageant

A long timpani roll . . . "Ladies and gentlemen, the sixty-fourth annual Miss America Pageant!"

I fought back tears. We'd heard this many times in practice, but this time it really meant something. I took my escorts' arms and followed the girl in front of us through the crowd to the end of the runway. I looked at the screaming crowd, the tight security, and felt like a prize boxer. The huge, huge wave of hype I'd felt as soon as we stepped out of the dressing room seemed now like it would engulf us. As I walked to my place between Debbye and Miss Illinois at the end of the runway, the press went crazy taking pictures. I smiled brilliantly, my mind racing.

"I must have made top ten," I thought. "Why else would they be taking so many pictures of me?"

I looked at my family. They sat in their usual place. They all smiled and waved at me, but I could tell they were crying. I didn't know how to interpret the tears. Were they crying because I didn't make top ten? Or were they crying because they were happy for me?

We circled the stage, each girl walking and waving to the audience. The introductions started. I again fought tears. The audience never stopped cheering between girls. I watched the TV monitors as each girl introduced herself.

"I can't believe people are watching this all over the world," I thought as the girl before me introduced herself.

I walked confidently to the mike.

"I'm Rebecca Eileen Trueblood, Miss Idaho!"

I followed the other girls around the stage and back into the lineup. We stood and waited for everyone to finish the introductions. Finally, all fifty-one girls stood in a line, waiting for the top ten to be announced. After a commercial break, the judges handed Gary Collins and Phyllis George the list.

"The top ten are chosen from the composite scores in interview, talent, swimsuit, and evening gown competitions. Preliminary competitions took place all week. The ten contestants on this list received the highest accumulative scores."

I could feel my hands getting sweaty. Finally, they opened the list and started reading.

"Here, in no particular order, are the top ten contestants. Miss Illinois . . ."

The crowd applauded loudly as Miss Illinois took her place in the winner's lineup.

"Miss Colorado . . ."

"Miss Washington, Jennifer Wahl!"

I started studying the lineup. I knew they wouldn't call two singers next to each other, or two pianists. I figured every third girl could be a singer.

"Miss Missouri, Debbye Turner!"

I watched the top ten girls grab each other's hands. Every time a slot for a singer came up, I tensed, ready for my name to be announced. I looked at the other girls still waiting to be called. One girl was an excellent pianist, another a harpist. One, two girls down, a very good singer.

It came down to the last spot, one I knew would be

filled by a singer. The announcer paused momentarily, and I waited for my name to be called.

"Miss Oklahoma . . . !"

I gasped, stunned. I just knew any second they'd announce there had been a mistake and they'd forgotten to call me. I couldn't believe it. Numbed, I turned and followed everyone else off stage. Nobody said a word.

The celebrity judges met and greeted each of us as we came off stage—Donald Trump, Phylicia Rashad, and Merv Griffin.

"You did great," they assured everyone. "We were really impressed by what you did."

I smiled and thanked them, but inside I wanted to tell them something different.

"No, I didn't," I wanted to say. "If I'd done well I would be out on stage with the winners!"

I couldn't think or feel. Numbly, we all walked back to the dressing room and changed into our robes. Stacy and I grabbed the bowl of popcorn we'd been eyeing earlier, poured melted chocolate over it, and sat silently in front of the TV watching the pageant. Neither of us said anything. We ate mechanically. I felt like a fog had descended and covered all of the girls. I stared at the TV screen, barely seeing it and not hearing a word. It felt like watching a program with the sound turned down.

"It's over and I'll never have a chance to do this again." I didn't think of the fact I was still Miss Idaho. Instead, I felt like every title had been stripped from me. I felt like plain old Becki, like I'd just lost something I'd worked for with all my heart.

No one cried; no one spoke. Mechanically we got ready for our next group number. I pasted a smile on my face as we stepped in front of the audience again. Friends and family all over the world were watching me. I didn't want to let them down or let them see how disappointed I felt.

The number ended, and we went back to sitting in front of the TV. We did another number, then came backstage and sat some more. I kept thinking of my family. I wanted to see them so badly, even though I knew as soon as I did I'd start crying.

The last number arrived, and we all went back on stage in our evening gowns. The top ten girls lined up for the final announcement of Miss America. The judges handed the results to Gary Collins.

"Third runner-up and the winner of an eleven-thousand-dollar scholarship is . . ." a drum rolled. ". . . Miss Illinois—Jeri Lynn Zimmerman!"

I watched the girl receive her flowers and felt numb inside. I didn't feel a part of the contest anymore. I just wanted it to be all over.

"Second runner-up is . . . Miss Colorado—Debbie Kiecks, winner of a fourteen-thousand-dollar scholarship!"

The second runner-up took her place and received her flowers.

"The role of the first runner-up is very important. Should Miss America be unable to perform her duties, the first runner-up will be called on to finish the year for her."

The audience waited expectantly.

"The first runner-up, and the winner of a twenty-thousand-dollar scholarship is . . . Miss Maryland—Virginia Cha!"

More applause, more tears. The girls left in the top ten lineup joined hands expectantly.

"The title of Miss America 1990 goes to . . ." another drum roll, ". . . Miss Missouri, Debbye Turner!"

I watched numbly as Debbye tearfully stood while the crown was placed on her head. Someone handed her a bouquet of flowers. She did her walk as the audience gave her a standing ovation. Inside I felt dead.

"This can't be real," I thought. "This is just a bad dream. I'm still going to win."

I watched Debbye finish the walk I'd been sure I was going to take. As soon as the TV cameras signed off, the press surrounded the girls. I fought my way to Debbye and gave her a hug and kiss. Everyone wanted to talk to her.

I worked my way to the edge of the crowd. A reporter came up to me, tape recorder in hand. "So, how does it feel to have come this far and lost?" she asked callously.

"Oh, it's OK," I lied. "I'm very happy for Debbye."

Inside I wanted to scream at her, "It hurts, OK? I've only poured all of myself into this for the last two years!" But I knew I couldn't say anything. I had to keep smiling, pretending.

The pageant officials moved us to the back room for the awards ceremony. Press people trailed along. I stood, outwardly smiling, inwardly with every part of me wanting to see my parents.

An announcer began handing out awards. After the talent award, he placed another trophy on the table in front of him.

"We're sorry this didn't get on the air. It's one of our most important awards." He paused as everyone waited for him to continue. "The award for Best Interview goes to Miss Idaho, Rebecca Eileen Trueblood."

I walked to the front, blinking back tears. I knew I had to smile, look happy for the award, but all I could think was that if I did so well in interview, I must have done horribly in talent.

I accepted the trophy, tears streaming down my cheeks. I hoped everyone thought I was happy for the award. Inside I felt twelve years old again, wanting my daddy to hold me.

Talent was the one thing I'd never been nervous about—the area that I'd always considered my area. I felt sick inside, knowing that I'd done my very, very best in talent and it hadn't been good enough.

The awards ceremony ended. Escorts let us into a large room where our families waited to see us.

"Daddy!" I whispered, tears streaming down my face.

I walked to my family and fell into my father's arms. The rest of the family circled around me. All of us cried.

"There were three top ten lists yesterday," Mom said brokenly. "I heard that you were on two of them."

"Oh, I hurt so much," I cried to myself as my dad held me close. I could feel him shaking as he cried with me.

For a few minutes we all stood and cried together. Finally I pulled away from my father and hugged everyone else. Even my brother, one of the strongest people in my life, couldn't stop his tears. I held up my trophy.

"I won Best Interview," I sniffled.

"Honey, that's great." Mom put her arms around me.

"Don't you realize?" I looked wildly at them. "I must have done horrible in talent. I did my best. I still didn't win." I stopped and gulped for air. "And I'll never be able to try this again."

I looked in their eyes. I could see so many denials they wanted to make, so many reassurances they wanted to give. But as they looked back at me, I think they knew nothing would help. We all stood holding each other. No one spoke.

Chapter **16**

A Dark Night

I left the convention center for the last time and let myself be escorted back to Trump Castle. I had stopped crying and once again felt numb.

The car stopped at the tower, and escorts whisked me through the lobby. The elevator stopped, and a group of men in suits, all centered around Donald Trump, got off.

"Mr. Trump, Mr. Trump, what do you think of this?"

The entourage of men jumped around Mr. Trump, all trying to get his attention at the same time. I stood and watched. I'd just started moving toward the elevator when Donald Trump spotted me. He stopped his group of men, silently.

"It's so nice to meet you, Rebecca." He reached out and took my hand. "I'm Donald Trump. You did such a beautiful job tonight, and I hope you enjoyed your stay. If I can do anything for you, please let me know."

With a smile he let go of my hand and moved down the hall, his group of men hastily following him. I got on the elevator, smiling to myself. "What a nice man," I thought. "And he even remembered my name!"

Upstairs in the room, Leanne said very little. She climbed in bed, and I went into the other room to think. Placing my trophy and corsage on the floor, I stared around me. Clothes lay strewn everywhere. Flowers and gifts from friends were also scattered around the room, mementos mixed in with everything else. I could feel my earlier numbness wearing away and the tears starting again.

"Why, God, why?" I whispered, looking at the room.

I saw the room-service menu sitting by the phone, and I grabbed it quickly. I'd been allotted twenty-five dollars a meal for the entire pageant. I'd hardly eaten a thing. I picked up the phone and dialed quickly.

"Hello? Room service? I'd like to get an order of fries, a piece of cheesecake, the turkey fruitplate, and a chocolate shake sent up to my room." I didn't care if they thought I was a glutton.

The food arrived half an hour later, and I sat in the middle of the floor, eating and trying to pack. Tears rolled down my face as I folded my rehearsal clothes. "Oh, Lord," I silently cried. "How could You let this happen? How could You have brought me so far and now nothing?"

No answer. Only silence. I reached for my interview outfit, my talent competition dress. Each article of clothing brought fresh tears. I packed the letters and cards from close friends, the photos of my week. And as I reached for another suitcase, I remembered my family's tears after tonight's pageant.

"God, how can this happen to my family? How can You let them go through this?"

I remembered the pain in my family's eyes, and I cried harder. And I wondered how I would face the people of Idaho.

"I've let them down too," I cried. Inside I felt like I wanted to apologize to the whole state. As I started packing my last suitcase, I tried to reason with myself. "Becki, you've come through a lot before with God's help. He'll help you through this too."

But inside, the pain didn't go away, and the words sounded empty and hollow. I looked out the window and watched the first streaks of dawn light the sky.

"Lord, help me to deal with this," I prayed. "I don't understand why this happened."

No answer. No peace. Finally, my belongings packed, my food eaten, I curled up on the floor, exhausted. Leanne woke me an hour later.

"Wake up, Becki, you'll miss your flight!"

I struggled awake. Morning light now flooded the room, and I looked around me, bewildered. In a flash the pageant came back, and I choked back tears. Inside I could feel a hard knot of pain. I went through the motions of getting ready and chatted cheerily with Leanne, and after breakfast, I went downstairs to meet my mother. She gave me a quick hug, and I could tell she hadn't gotten much rest the night before either.

We climbed into a taxi, and as we drove through the streets of Atlantic City I felt stunned. In one night, all traces of the pageant had been removed! It looked like it had never happened. All the lighted signs had been changed, all the banners were gone. My eyes filled. How could it happen so fast?

Mom patted my hand. "It's OK, honey."

I knew she felt what I felt. Once again I saw her pain and felt the now-familiar twisting of guilt inside me. How could I have done this to her?

As we arrived at the airport, I wondered what the rest of my family was thinking. They'd be going back to Idaho while Mom and I went to Washington, D.C., for a few days. What would their reception be in Boise? I felt glad I didn't have to go home yet.

We flew to Washington, D.C., and visited the Idaho senators and representatives. Inside I still felt numbed pain. I smiled and kept my happy façade intact the entire visit, though. The centennial coordinators and I made plans for the upcoming Idaho Centennial celebration. They congratulated me on my interview award, but inside I wanted to die. People told me the pageant results were due to politics. It didn't matter. I felt empty; I had nothing else to give. I knew I should have been proud of the interview award, but it didn't mean anything. It didn't get me into top ten.

On the flight home to Boise I went over and over everything in my mind. I knew I couldn't have done more than I had. I had done my best, but it still wasn't good enough. I tried to think of what I'd done wrong but couldn't find any answers. I hoped once I had a chance to sleep and physically recuperate that I'd feel better. I still felt the exhaustion of those two frantic weeks.

My mother and I talked little about the pageant. I didn't feel I could burden her with my feelings when I knew she was struggling so much with her own. And I tried to pray. "Why, Lord, why?"

There never seemed to be an answer.

I arrived back home and found myself approached constantly by people who wanted to talk about the pageant. The day after I came home, a woman stopped me in the supermarket. "The competition must have been really rough back there," she commiserated.

I smiled and agreed, but inside I wanted to say, "No, it wasn't that rough. I just wasn't what they wanted this year." But I knew I couldn't say anything.

People kept approaching. Some expressed anger. "It wasn't fair!"

Yet even though I agreed with them, I had to keep smiling, pretending that nothing mattered as much as it did. Most people were wonderful, but inside I didn't want wonderful. I felt so guilty for letting everyone down that I just wanted to apologize.

One woman saw the pain in my eyes.

"You're our Miss America," she told me.

My eyes welled with tears, and she tried to comfort me some more. I wanted to say, "No, I'm not Miss America. I'm Miss Idaho."

Everywhere I went, people wanted to help me get through the pain and disappointment. I wanted to get through it on my own, and that made me feel guilty too.

I had a hard time leaving the house. I slept lots, cried often, and watched TV. Every night I dreamed about the pageant. Every morning I woke up with it on my mind. I began to wonder if it would ever leave me. After having Miss America as my focus for so long, I didn't know how to deal with it being over. All I wanted to do was curl up on the couch, shades closed, and avoid taking phone calls. People came to the house and I couldn't open the door. I always felt I had to explain why I didn't win, and I was so tired of trying to figure it out myself.

"Lord," I prayed. "I've always felt that I handled things well in the past. I can't handle this. Please help me feel better. Please help me understand."

No answer. All my prayers seemed to reach no farther than the ceiling. For the first time in my life, I felt deserted by God. I remembered how I'd been taught as a small child to "ask, and receive." "When two or three are gathered together in My name . . ." All along I'd asked and prayed, but now everything I'd always believed in had been ripped out from under me.

Days went by. A week. I wanted to hide. My depression seemed to get worse instead of better. I carried a dull, achy feeling with me everywhere. And I didn't feel I could talk to anyone. Being Miss Idaho, I couldn't say anything negative about my experience, and I didn't want to come across as a sore loser. My family tried to help, but they struggled with their own disappointment.

"Oh, God, if I hadn't done this, my family wouldn't be going through this now."

Everyone hurt so badly for me. I remembered all the people who'd donated time and money to me. I felt I'd let them down. I wanted to run from the guilt, but I couldn't. There was nowhere to go.

Three weeks after the pageant I went to California to visit friends. I felt that if I got away from Idaho for a while I'd be able to heal. I wanted so badly to sit down with them, just talk, and have them tell me that they really understood. But no one could really understand. I knew that, and I felt bad.

My friends reached out to me, trying to help. I kept remembering how all I'd told them the year before was "I'm busy." They kept giving and giving all year. I didn't want them to have to give any more.

I began to question God's reasoning. I'd been praying and praying for peace, healing. He never seemed to answer. "God, I want to trust You, but this is hard. This is really, *really* hard for me."

Still no answer. I returned to Idaho feeling no better than when I left. It felt weird to know that no one could really understand my feelings.

"Why are you so upset about a beauty pageant?" I could see them thinking.

I couldn't explain it. I couldn't make them understand that I'd put my very best on the line for Miss America. I'd worked harder than I'd ever worked in my life. And I'd lost.

People called, asking me to speak in schools. I didn't feel I could do it. I felt so achy and sick inside I didn't feel I had anything to say. I wondered if I'd ever be a normal person again.

"This is so stupid," I raged inwardly. "How can two weeks of my life affect me so much? Why can't I get beyond this?" "Lord, if this had to happen, why did I have to fail in such a *big* way? All along I've prayed for Your will. All along I've prayed that if I didn't win, You'd help me handle it. I'm not handling it very well, Lord. Why aren't You helping me?"

No reply. No answer. Only the dull achy feeling I feared I'd live with for the rest of my life.

Chapter **17**

Best for Me?

The invitation to Debbye Turner's homecoming arrived in the mail. I knew Debbye's executive director and mine had discussed it already. Mom handed it to me, a neutral look on her face. I read through it quickly.

". . . invited to join me in my homecoming celebration . . ."

Mom looked at me. "Are you going to go?"

I looked again at the invitation. Maybe it would be good for me. Maybe it would help to see Debbye again.

"I don't know," I replied slowly.

I decided to go. I steeled myself for the four days of events. I knew all the bigwigs from Miss America would be there, and because this was her state, the people would naturally gravitate to her.

I arrived in Missouri, settled into the bed-and-breakfast, and immediately began the series of events and parties. Miss Montana and all the top ten girls had also been invited. Out of the top ten, however, only Miss Colorado and Miss Arkansas accepted the invitation. Miss Montana and I were the only two who scheduled all four days of the celebration. After Miss Colorado and Miss Arkansas went back home, the two of us found we were just there—watchers of the excitement rather than part of it.

Even though Debbye was really, really busy, she

seemed her old self. I felt so honored to have been asked back for her celebration. She did everything to make Miss Montana and me feel welcome. But this was *her* celebration, not ours, and I fought tears the entire time.

People came up to me, smiles on their faces, saying hurtful things, like, "We knew it was Debbye from the start. Nobody else had a chance against her."

I smiled, trying to be really strong, but inside I hurt deeply. I wanted to tell these people how I'd worked just as hard as Debbye had. I felt happy for her, but I wanted it too.

"God, please help me make it through this," I prayed at night. "This is really, really hard for me. Help me not to be jealous of what Debbye has."

I knew when I got home a stack of bills would be waiting for me. Glittery gowns, manicures, haircuts—these things all cost money. I had been debt free going into the pageant. Now I owed money to what felt like half the state of Idaho. I didn't know where I'd get the money to pay everyone back.

Every day I watched Debbye travel in a limousine and get lots of money for each appearance. Everyone wanted a part of her. She spoke, giving the same message I'd always known I'd give as Miss America: "You can be anything if you work hard enough for it. Even if you come from nothing you can make something of yourself. Believe in yourself. Reach for your goals."

As I listened to Debbye speak, I felt a hollowness inside. Would I ever believe those words again? I'd worked harder than I'd ever worked for something and I didn't receive it. It was a lie. The whole thing was a lie.

I watched Debbye say, do, experience, and be everything I'd wanted so badly. I felt like God was slapping me in the face: "I'm sorry, I'm not giving you this desire. You can have any other desire but not this one."

I smiled my way through the rest of the four days. On the last day I noticed Gussie Turner, Debbye's mother, watching me closely. I tried to keep smiling, but tears always threatened.

"Oh, please stop looking at me," I silently pleaded. I knew that if she said anything I'd start crying.

She kept watching. At supper that night I tried to act normal and happy. She kept looking at me and grabbing my hand. I kept fighting tears. Conversation continued around us.

". . . Yes, I'll be headed to Atlanta next week . . ."

"Please stop grabbing my hand," I pleaded silently.

She squeezed my hand again. I felt tears threatening to overflow. She must have seen them, because she got out of her chair and put her arm around me. I couldn't hold in the tears any longer. "Please don't believe I'm not happy for Debbye," I sobbed. "I am. I'm so proud of her. It's just *so hard*. I wanted what she has so badly."

She held me tight and let me cry. "Lord," she began praying. "Becki's hurting right now and she really needs Your healing touch. Please touch her now with Your love."

I continued to cry as she held me. Finally, after several minutes, she spoke again.

"Becki, God has great plans for you, and He doesn't want you to be ruined by this Miss America thing." She stopped for a second, then continued. "You know, I always knew that if Debbye got close enough she could take the crown. But I know your parents felt the same way."

I continued crying. She smoothed my hair.

"I just want you to know I'll be looking for your name later on."

She held me until I stopped crying. I wanted to tell her that her encouragement had made everything better, but the pain refused to leave.

I flew back home to Idaho, still not feeling any healing. A few of my suitcases still sat packed in the corner of my room. I'd been unable to face the memories they held when I arrived home from Atlantic City. One afternoon I determined to unpack those last three suitcases. I had to get beyond this. I felt so selfish. All the time and money that had gone into the pageant should have been spent on something more important. I felt sorry for myself, and I hated it. I hauled the suitcases to the bed and opened the first one resolutely.

Cards, books, and letters spilled out. I sifted through the memories, tears streaming down my face. The ache inside felt like it would devour me. I picked up one letter. "We're praying for you," it said. "God has a plan for your life."

I cried harder. How could this happen when so many people were praying for me? A book slid off the pile. I picked it up. "Miss America Pageant, 1990!" All the girls, the sponsors, the parties. I looked through the commemorative book and sobbed. How could two weeks affect me so much?

The clothes, pictures, more letters. Each new discovery added to the pain and growing anger I felt. How could God let this happen?

"Becki, are you all right?"

I turned quickly and saw my mother standing at the door of my room. Suddenly all the pain and anger seemed too much, and all the emotion I'd been bottling inside for so long exploded out of me. "I just don't understand!" I yelled. "It makes me mad!" I swept up a handful of letters and waved them in front of me. "Look at these letters, telling me God called me to be Miss America. People I respect wrote these! Why isn't God leading? I just don't understand!"

Mom watched me yell, tears in her eyes. When my

anger finally dissolved into tears again, she answered. "Becki, we prayed for God's will to be done in your life. God's will *was* done. It wasn't the will *you* wanted, or the will *I* wanted, but it was *God's* will. His will was accomplished through all this."

I sat on the bed and cried. All the fight was gone out of me. Mom sat down beside me, put her arms around me, and cried with me. I kept thinking about what she'd said.

"God's will *was* accomplished. God's will *was* accomplished."

I wanted to believe it with every part of me.

Chapter 18

Realization

The pain got easier to handle. I still struggled with God, but I tried to go on. I couldn't let it kill me.

I began accepting speaking engagements again. I knew if I was going to get rid of the negative feelings, I had to give more of myself, and if I wanted to be a busy Miss Idaho, I had to do it myself. I sent letters and called TV stations, hospitals, and schools, letting everyone know I was available to speak.

Mom's words kept going around in my mind. "God's will *was* accomplished . . . God's will *was* accomplished."

I started speaking to schools and business groups. My message had changed only a little from before. I still encouraged people to work for what they wanted, but I also told them that life doesn't play favorites. Hard times will hit everyone, and it's what a person does after the tough times that makes a difference.

Each public appearance ended with a song. I chose to sing "Best for Me." With every performance, I found myself having to believe my own words.

"Here I stand with my life in Your hands
It's funny how You make Your love appear.
Gone away, You dried all my tears
Took away all my fears . . . Time and time again
You've made it all so clear . . . that

You know what's best for me . . .
You want what's best for me
There may be times when I can't see
The plans You hold for my life.
When the answers seem far away
I know now just to trust and pray
It took some time, but now I believe . . .
You know what's best for me . . ."[1]

Each time I spoke the words of encouragement, every time I sang my song, I came closer to believing it myself. I found myself trusting God again. I didn't understand why it had to happen, but I knew, somehow, He had a plan.

Just before Christmas, I spoke at a grade school outside of Boise. Bright-eyed children looked at my crown and banner, and I could see their own dreams shining in their eyes. I reached out to them with my hands and my heart. I wanted each child to know he or she was loved. I wanted to show them I really, really cared; that a title didn't have to go to my head.

"You are a special person just as you are," I told one little girl.

"Never stop trying for what you want. Never let bad things stop you from following your dreams," I told a young boy.

I spoke my words of encouragement and sang my song. Before I left, I gave each child a hug.

I climbed in my car, took off my crown and banner, and drove to my next appointment.

"At least I don't have to wear the crown at my next appearance," I thought as I maneuvered my way through traffic. I only wore the banner and crown when speaking to children. When I spoke to adults I tried to present a different side of the pageant world.

I hummed as I drove. "You gave me time . . . time to

work this whole thing through, and I found that I was nothing here without You."

My mother's words came back to me. "God's will *was* accomplished. God's will *was* accomplished."

I stopped humming as the realization hit me. "God, I'm beginning to see reasons why I didn't win." I didn't realize I'd spoken out loud until my own voice startled me.

I thought of how I'd always wanted to sing professionally, but I never knew what I'd say to people in concerts. My life had been very good—all along God had blessed me. I always wondered if I'd have anything to say. How could people who hurt relate to my relatively easy life?

But now, after losing the pageant, I felt I could instantly relate to people who had worked with all of themselves for something and lost. Maybe everyone hadn't experienced Miss America, but many, *many* people had experienced the loss I felt. I knew I could take in their feelings and experiences, and people would have a connection with me.

For the first time since the Miss America Pageant, I felt at peace. The hurt remained, but I knew I'd be able to keep it in a tiny corner of myself. I had a reason. I could heal.

"Thank You, Lord," I whispered. "Thank You."

---

1. Phil Silas, "Best for Me," © 1987 by Socorro Songs, Sacramento, California.

Chapter 19

Miss Idaho 1990

"Ladies and gentlemen, the forty-first annual centennial Miss Idaho Pageant!"

The curtain rose to the applause of the audience. Music started, and I began to sing. All around me on stage the new contestants for the Miss Idaho crown danced and sang.

". . . let's celebrate Idaho . . ."

I looked at their red, white, and blue dresses as we sang. Each girl looked as nervous and excited as I'd felt the year before. I couldn't believe it had been a year.

The number ended, and we all walked backstage. I changed into my evening gown while the contestants introduced themselves to the audience. I'd just reached the stage again when I heard the hosts, Gene Hill and Debra Sue Maffit, Miss America 1983, announcing my name.

I walked into the spotlight, smiling at the audience. Stopping at the end of the small runway, I stood and waved. The audience applauded continuously. I turned and walked to the center of the stage, where my brother Todd surprised me by walking onstage and handing me a rose. I hugged him tightly, waved again to the audience, and walked offstage.

After a commercial, I knew, the top eight would be announced. Once again I remembered how excited I'd been last year. Now one of the girls on stage would be taking my place as the reigning Miss Idaho.

I paced a corner backstage and thought back over my year. After Christmas, I'd thrown myself into being Miss Idaho with a fervor I never thought I could feel again. I spoke to people and tried to show them a different side of the pageant world. I tried to lay my life open for everyone to see. I'd given it my very best.

Onstage I heard a long drum roll and Debra Sue Maffit reading the top eight contestants. The audience cheered wildly after each name was announced. After the last girl had joined the winner's lineup, the judges were introduced. All the top eight contestants ran around backstage to prepare for the swimsuit/physical fitness contest. Onstage, the last judge was introduced, and Debra began singing.

Debra Sue Maffit, Miss America 1983. I wondered what her year as Miss America had been like. Debbye Turner and I had stayed in touch all year. I remembered Debbye coming to Moscow, Idaho, for the jazz festival. We got to talk, just the two of us. And after listening to her, I realized all the struggles I had on a local level, she had—greatly magnified—on the national level. I felt better knowing the job of Miss America wasn't perfect, that Debbye had had rough times too.

Debra finished her song, and the audience responded enthusiastically. Gene Hill began talking about the swimsuit competition. Debra joined him again at the podium. From backstage I watched the eight semifinalists model their swimsuits for the judges and audience. I remembered my own feelings of nervousness last year and felt for the girls as they carefully walked the stage. As the last girl finished her walk, Debra Sue Maffit started speaking.

"Let's bring the reigning Miss Idaho, Rebecca Eileen Trueblood, out here!"

I hurried from my place backstage to the podium and

stood between the two hosts. I hoped I didn't look too surprised—this wasn't planned as part of the program. Debra smiled at me, the audience, then continued. "I've gotten to spend a lot of time with Becki over the last few days, and I have to say, she's a class act!"

The audience responded with loud cheering. I blushed and thanked her.

"Do you remember what it feels like to win Miss Idaho?" she asked me.

"I feel so much for the girls," I replied. "And whoever the winner is, the next two to three hours will be wonderful and exciting. But tomorrow morning when she wakes up, she'll realize, like I did, that she's representing an entire state of people. It's a huge responsibility."

Debra nodded in agreement. The audience applauded.

"Tell us, Becki, what are some of your future plans?" Debra asked.

"Well." I laughed slightly. "For the next two months I want to do nothing. I want to water-ski, lie in the sun, spend time with friends—all the things I haven't had time to do for so long. In August I'd like to do some more motivational speaking and pursue my music further."

"And what a great singer you are!" Debra said, smiling.

I thanked her again and smiled at the audience.

"Miss Idaho, 1989, Rebecca Eileen Trueblood!" Gene announced.

I smiled and walked backstage again. All activity stopped on stage for another commercial break. Backstage the semifinalists rushed around preparing for the talent competition. I returned to the dressing room and changed into my long blue talent dress. As I stood in front of the mirror I remembered how my confidence in my singing had slowly returned after Christmas. I knew, in myself, that I had done a good job back at Miss America. My voice might not have been what the judges were looking for, but it didn't mean I couldn't sing. Slowly, lovingly, God had helped me heal in that area too.

The girls rushed around me, preparing for talent. I listened as the first girl began her number onstage. I walked to a quiet corner backstage and quietly sang through my song. Another girl started her talent number, then another. It seemed to be going so fast. As the last girl finished her number, I heard my name announced again.

"And now, performing the song she did in Atlantic City, here's your reigning Miss Idaho, Rebecca Eileen Trueblood!"

I walked into the spotlight, microphone in hand. My familiar tape started, and I began singing. I walked the stage slowly as I poured myself into the song. As I came to the end, I raised one hand in the air. The audience erupted in applause. I bowed, waved, and left the stage.

"Thanks, God," I whispered as I came offstage.

While I changed for the Idaho centennial number, the contestants, dressed in evening gowns, did a dance. After they finished, the Treasure Valley cloggers performed a rousing dance. I came back onstage just as they finished. I stood in the center of the stage in a modern white dress with girls in old-fashioned clothes on one side, girls in modern clothes on the other.

". . . let's celebrate Idaho . . ."

I felt every word as I sang. I felt so proud of Idaho— to have been able to represent the people of Idaho for an entire year. They loved, supported, and believed in me. So many people had donated so much time and money to me. And I knew that wherever I went in my life, the people of Idaho would be in my heart.

The song ended. I rushed back to the dressing room to change into my evening gown again. The contestants busily changed into their gowns too. I faced my final walk as Miss Idaho. One of them would very shortly be taking her first walk as Miss Idaho. I felt ready to pass on the crown. A month ago, I felt I wanted to hang on to it forever. And had I been given the option then to keep it another year, I probably would have. But now, as I prepared for my farewell walk, I realized I was ready to let go. I felt excited to face the next stage of my life.

On the stage, Debra Sue Maffit sang another song. I finished changing and retouching my hair and makeup, then stood backstage waiting to hear my name announced again. Debra's song ended, there was a brief pause as she walked back to the podium, then I heard my cue.

"Ladies and gentlemen, let's stand and welcome your reigning Miss Idaho, Rebecca Eileen Trueblood, as she does her farewell walk."

The audience rose and applauded as I walked onstage. Over the sound system I could hear my prerecorded voice: "There aren't words to express how I feel tonight. Being Miss Idaho has given me memories I will cherish forever."

I walked slowly down the runway, smiling and waving.

"This year has been extremely exciting, but it's also been a huge responsibility. I always wanted people to look beyond the banner and crown and see a real person. I wanted people to realize we can make a difference with our lives."

I finished the runway and now walked the stage.

"There are so many people I want to thank—too many for me to be able to mention every one of you. But I want to thank my board members. You've given so much of yourselves for me. Thank you."

As I walked, I remembered how my board began trusting my judgment as they got to know me better. With their support, I felt able to speak on issues I really care about.

"Thank you, Tom, Leanne, Amy, and Eric. You've taken me into your homes and made me feel like family. Thank you, sponsors. Your support makes the Miss Idaho Pageant possible. Thank you, family and friends. You've supported and loved me all along."

I reached a set of stairs on the stage and climbed them slowly.

"Especially, I would like to thank my mom and dad. You've always believed, always listened, always loved. Most important, you've given me a firm foundation on which to build my life—a belief in our God."

I stood smiling at the audience. I thought of how my mother had helped me stay busy as Miss Idaho. She fielded calls, wrote letters, and basically kept me organized. She and Dad loved me unconditionally.

"And to my brother, Todd. I'm so proud of you. I love you. Thank you for believing in me."

I remembered how Todd and I had become so much closer during my year as Miss Idaho. He stopped being a sibling to fight with and became the strongest brother I could ever wish for.

"Thank you, the people of Idaho, for giving me this opportunity. I've loved my year as your representative. Now, as I give another girl the privilege of representing you, I think of this not as an ending but as a beginning to the next phase of my life. Thank you all."

My tape ended, the audience applauded, and I waved my final farewell. In a few minutes I'd be taking the crown off my head and placing it on another girl's. Inside I felt at peace. The year as Miss Idaho provided me with so much growth. I lost my childhood illusion of believing God had only one purpose for my life. Now I knew that God had many plans for my life. And I could hardly wait to see where He would lead me next.

" . . . You know what's best for me . . . "

I turned and left the stage, walking, not to an ending, but to the beginning of God's new plans for me.